ADOPTION
without fear

Edited by
James L. Gritter, M.S.W.

Corona Publishing Company
San Antonio 1989

Library of Congress Cataloging-in-Publication Data

Adoption without fear / edited by James L. Gritter.
        p.   cm.
    Bibliography: p.
    ISBN 0-931722-71-3 : $7.95
    1. Adoption--United States--Case studies.   I. Gritter, James L.,
1950-   .
HV875.55.A365   1989
362.7'34--dc19   88-72307
                                                                            CIP

10   9   8   7   6   5

Printed and bound in the United States of America

In Memory Of

The Hon. Kenneth J. Mackness
Judge of Probate
Grand Traverse County, Michigan

For his dedication and support of open adoption,
and for his special sensitivity
to all those whose lives
are touched by adoption

A Note From The Publisher

In 1983, Kathleen Silber and Phylis Speedlin came to us with a book they had self-published in a small edition. It was called *Dear Birthmother* and it emphasized the role of the biological parents in the "adoption triangle." It suggested that happier families would result from the elimination of secrecy and closed records. The idea of open adoption was very new, they said, and still very controversial.

I had never had any direct contact with the adoption process. When I finished reading the book, I had only one question: How could it be that an idea so obviously sensible and humane was considered controversial, even shocking? Was it really true that only one or two agencies in the U.S. were actively involved in open adoption procedures? The authors assured me that this was so.

We published the book. During the following years, its influence grew steadily as thousands of adoptive couples discovered that openness gives deeper meaning to the adoption process—and that, contrary to accepted opinion, it actually *removes* many of the fears associated with adoption. Today, scores of agencies in the U.S., Canada, and overseas offer the option of openness.

The book you are holding brings together the emotional first-person accounts of seventeen families who have taken this option. Several of the contributors to *Adoption Without Fear* have shared the birth experience with their child's biological parents. Others have had less intimate contact with the birthparents but still found that openness enriches their lives in ways they never thought possible. While the emotional risks are certainly greater, all have been ultimately thrilled with the experience and are now secure in their role as parents. "Love has been doubled, not divided," is the way one parent puts it. This book emerged because a group of adoptive parents, gathered to prepare themselves for a second adoption, were convinced that others could draw strength from their experiences. We agreed, and that opportunity is yours now.

David Bowen

Cover: Birthparents Amy and Dan *(left)* with Mike
and Jean Spry, and their child, Ian

1. Lee and Robin Cottrell with Autumn

2. Mike and Jean Spry with Judge Mackness
holding Lara

3. Cathy and Doug Lundy with Matthew and
birthmother Brenda

4. Jean Spry with birthmom Reneé, little Lara,
and Reneé's mother, Penny

5. Aaron Tonn with birthmom Jennifer *(right)*,
her mother and a cousin

6. Birthmother Amy with Ian at the Spry home

7. The Olsons' Davey holding Jayme, 18 hours old

8. Don and Kathy Spinniken with baby
Matthew and Lynette

CONTENTS

Adoption Without Fear

Introduction

As a rookie social worker fresh out of graduate school in 1974, how could I have known much better? I presumed the professional prescription for appropriate adoption practices had been well thought through and I mindlessly accepted them. I was impressed with the conscientious attitudes adoption workers brought to their work and, as a result, I was confident we were all on the right track.

Adoption was that happy bit of social work by which "unwanted" children were placed with highly deserving, infertile, middle-class couples. Solving two painful problems in one efficient transaction, adoption was something to feel good about. What's more, adoption workers could count on well-behaved, eager-to-please clients who were generally quick to defer to the worker's all-powerful position. And if that weren't enough, the adoption worker could expect to have his or her storklike role remembered with chocolate chip windfalls at the holiday time of year. What could be better?

Slowly, though, misgivings grew and after a while even multiplied. As I listened to my clients, I began to sense that things were not as simple as they had first appeared. My first set of misgivings had to do with birthparents. Professional wisdom, at the time, held that they were a pathological client group. Pregnancy out of wedlock was automatically viewed as a manifestation of unconscious hostility. Conventional wisdom held that birthparents were uncaring, wild, reckless, promiscuous, and usually from the wrong side of the tracks. As such, they were considered highly unstable; there could be no doubt that their children were better off without them. The pain associated with adoption was justifiable, for they were only reaping the just consequences of their behavior.

It didn't take long, however, for me to notice that the birthparents I met were not the people they were reputed to be. As a matter of fact, in all my diverse caseload, they were easily the most impressive clients. They were bright, caring, and surprisingly mature. I was awestruck by their capacity to sacrifice their most fervent, personal hopes for the sake of advancing the life chances of their children. I found their willingness to trust me with the future of their children completely unnerving. It occurred to me in no uncertain terms that these fine people surely deserved to be treated with dignity and respect. (Only later, I am ashamed to admit, did I come to realize that even if they were not so impressive, they still deserved respect and dignity.)

My next wave of misgivings involved adoptees. Everything in adoption was justified with the phrase "best interests of the child." It reached a point where every time I heard the phrase, I would immediately translate it in my mind to "best interests of the adoptive parents." How could it be good for children to lie to them about issues central to their sense of identity and deny them a sense of rootedness? When searching adoptees came to us completely preoccupied with and devoting all their life energy to learning about their origins, it was difficult to take refuge in that hollow phrase "best interests."

I also had misgivings about the interaction between adoptive parents and agencies. There were so many games built into the process that there were actually books written for adoptive parents instructing them how to play the game well. I was puzzled at the hostility one could sense lurking behind some of the smiling, compliant faces of adoptive parents. How was it possible that the persons so clearly designated to benefit from the process were so obviously irritated with it and eager to be done with it?

It did not take a wizard to ascertain that drastic changes were called for. Fortunately my agency, Community, Family and Children Services, was not afraid of change. In fact, workers were encouraged to think, to be innovative, and to advocate for their clients. Proposed changes were thought through very carefully, implemented little by little, and evaluated by a process of painstaking review. As a staff, we sensed immediately that we were on a more honest and, therefore, more promising course. We no longer felt as though we were accomplices to an insidious process.

In 1980, after spending some invaluable time with our gracious friends at Catholic Social Services in Green Bay, Wisconsin, we took the plunge and changed our philosophical approach from confidential adoption to open adoption. We decided to do adoption *with* people, not *to* them. That meant moving birthparents and adoptive parents out of their traditional passive roles and encouraging them to truly participate in and take charge of this life event which could effect them so profoundly.

In confidential adoption all the effort is directed toward separating people as completely as possible. It presumes that birthparents and adoptive parents are natural adversaries. Open adoption, on the other hand, sees no advantage in severing all ties between the families. It recognizes that all the parties involved are inextricably interconnected and that it is impossible to disconnect them from each other emotionally, medically, or psychologically. Open adoption seeks to make happy use of this interconnectedness. It assumes that birthparents and adoptive parents are likely to respect each other once they have met and shared their stories. Once a genuine sense of compatibility is established, they are well able to plan for the adoption in a spirit of mutual appreciation and concern.

The two forms of adoption are different in their handling of the fears which accompany the experience. Anxiety is intrinsic to adoption because the process requires so much interdependence and because the stakes are so high. In confidential adoption, secrecy is employed to insulate the adoptive parents from the birthparents in the hope of muting the anxiety. What starts out as an effort to minimize the tension ultimately creates a long-term anxiety since it is so difficult to come to terms with the unknown. The secrecy breeds a low-grade paranoia. Open adoption, on the other hand, meets the fear head on. When adoptive parents sit in the same room with birthparents and negotiate a plan for adoption, they face the specter of disapproval and rejection. When they welcome a child into their home and hearts prior to the legal relinquishment of parental rights, they are completely vulnerable and risk a loss that resembles the very loss experienced by birthparents. They are able to take these risks because, after careful consideration of the issues, they believe people really are capable of cooperation and integrity. Once the risks are successfully weathered, the adoptive parents are liberated from the insidious fear of the unknown.

When we announced to our clients that we had modified our policies, we expected that the changes would be warmly received by birthparents but possibly would meet a cooler response from adoptive parents. In fact, to be perfectly honest, we were concerned that our policy change would repel potential adoptive parents, a situation which, in the extreme, would leave us with no resources for the children entrusted to our care. Our concerns were magnified when some of the prospective adoptive parents already in our system protested our switch which for them was midstream and irksome. Over time, however, we have been delighted to discover that the people who are most enthusiastic about open adoption are our adoptive parents. As the following accounts will show, they have become the most vocal supporters of open adoption.

The route to acceptance of open adoption is varied. Some prospective adoptive parents immediately recognize in it something which connects to their view of life. It seems more "natural" to them. They sense, in open adoption, the Golden Rule in action and it pleases them. Some people approaching us have told us that until they encountered this cooperative approach to adoption, adoption held no appeal for them. They told us that they could not participate in a process where they would have the guilt of gaining so enormously at the expense of someone else's devastating loss unless they could give something back. The modest return they wish to offer to birthparents is respect and reassurance.

Not all of our adoptive parents are immediately enthusiastic about openness. Probably most of our prospective parents approach us "intrigued but wary." Those are the families that benefit the most from the agency's educational program. (See Afterword for a description of the educational program and an explanation of Michigan law.) Given a well-thought-out rationale for openness expressed by enthusiastic adoption professionals, most families find their fears relieved and are freed to enjoy and share the positive, embracing energy within them. They develop a heart for birthparents.

Some potential adoptive parents indeed are repelled by openness and sometimes that is just as well. Those people who seek to *own* a child, for example, see no appeal in open adoption. Since we believe an attitude of ownership is incompatible with successful adoption, we are relieved when openness prompts such prospects to try their chances elsewhere. We are sad, though, when loving people shy away because they lack the self-confidence necessary for openness. The point of these stories, however, is that openness certainly does not repel all prospective adoptive parents. This is an important fact to establish because a certain number of adoption professionals, repelled by openness for their own reasons, attempt to dismiss the prospect of open adoption on the basis that "adoptive parents will never buy it." Their assumption is clearly erroneous, and it is one of the major purposes of this book to refute it.

It is not easy to describe the sort of adoptive parents who enjoy open adoption. The usual socioeconomic terms we use to describe and categorize people don't seem to apply. It is not a matter of formal education, wealth, or religion that leads them to embrace openness; rather it is a matter of concern and respect for others that qualifies them for openness.

For all their many diversities, our adoptive families share at least six important commonalities.

1. They tend to see the world in positive terms. They believe win–win solutions are possible and they aspire to them.
2. They genuinely like other people and are able to identify with them. They do not automatically see others as threatening but instead are excited at the idea of expanding their social system.
3. They are open-minded. Everyone fancies himself open-minded,

but these good people truly are. They are willing to consider new possibilities.

4. They are self-confident and willing to take risks. They enjoy taking independent action and are able to improvise when necessary.
5. They accept the fact that adoption is different from having children born to them. They are enthusiastic about the child's prior heritage.
6. They do not see children as possessions. They do not seek to own children but rather realize that children are meant to be loved and nurtured as they mature and grow toward independence.

We are proud of our adoptive parents. We can't take much credit for them since they developed the aforementioned attitudes well before they contacted us, but we can and do relish our association with them. Without their understanding and integrity, we would be stymied in our effort to offer birthparents a form of adoption they can live with comfortably. Our program is only as good as the adoptive parents who carry out its ideals.

We receive many calls from would-be adoptive parents beyond the geographic boundaries of our service area and it is soon clear from our conversations with them that many of them possess these same impressive attitudes. We believe the families, given some encouragement and opportunity, would be fully able to enter loving relationships with the birthfamilies choosing them. We hope these vignettes will bolster their efforts to make openness more widely available.

With rare exception, it has been our pleasure to observe involvement in our program affect our participants in positive ways. We have seen people grow as a result of their experience of "living on the edge." They become braver, more self-confident, and as a result seem to live with more enthusiasm. Many report they have grown in their faith which they found sustaining in their most anxious times. Still others have learned a great deal about what it means to see the world through someone else's eyes. Our participants all add to their families, and most of them add lasting friends as well. Some of our people even gain a cause. They have found their passions so stirred by their adoption experience that they feel a responsibility to assist in furthering this social movement. It's really quite amazing to see what can happen when we social workers learn to trust the people we serve.

This book emerged when a group of adoptive parents were brought together to prepare themselves for a second adoption. They were eager to share their experiences, and as they heard each other's stories, they seemed to grasp immediately the power these stories collectively had. It was decided that the time had come to write a book. They knew that even as they had drawn strength from each other, so could many others.

A notice was sent to our adoptive parents inviting them to share their experiences. The chapters in this book are the result of that invitation. The content of these chapters has in no substantial way been altered. They contain tears of anguish and of joy. They are a tribute to what love, candor, and courage can accomplish. They demonstrate that, in an atmosphere of support, respect, and honesty, it is fully possible to experience adoption without fear.

James L. Gritter, M.S.W.
Child Welfare Supervisor

Julie* and Ric Vander Haagen

"Love is doubled, not divided"

As my husband Ric and I were preparing to attend the adoption orientation meeting, we were tense and anxious about what to expect of this first step into the world of adoption. We felt we were going to "meet the competition"—other couples just as eager to start their families. Ric has a deep aversion to pretense of any sort and his distaste for suits is formidable, but he decided reluctantly that making a good impression was much more important than his liking of unpretentious clothing. He decided to wear his baby blue three-piece suit; I decided on my baby pink dress.

I took too long in getting ready, which delayed us and we arrived a few minutes late. This added to our tension since we were certain the agency would deem our tardiness a negative factor. Once we had settled into some seats, we surveyed the room around us. We were depressed to see at least fifty other couples there to receive the same information we sought. The fact that most of them wore casual clothing was not lost on Ric, and we shared an anxious glance. Not only would we be viewed as tardy, we would also be seen as uptight.

We left the meeting discouraged. It looked like we were in for a slow process and we were concerned about the impression we had made. Our mood on the way home was bleak. It was at that low point that we noticed a vivid rainbow arching gracefully over the road ahead of us. We knew that to be a sign of God's promises

*The name of the writer of the chapter appears first in each case.

and our tense mood was replaced with renewed hope.

That hope was realized in 1980, only one year later, when we adopted Sara in the agency's first open adoption (a fact, by the way, of which Sara is very proud). It was the agency's educational program that prepared us for openness. We came to realize through the year of meetings with the agency that it was important for our children to know where they came from, why they were adopted, and that they were loved by their birthfamilies as much as our families would love and cherish them. We believed in this concept of openness and decided to "take the plunge." We knew that we were challenging traditional processes of adoption and that we would receive comments of dismay and disagreement. Fortunately, our families and friends found the process interesting and were very supportive.

At the same time we were settling into a desire for openness, the agency was working with an unusually mature single mother who was eight months pregnant. Phoebe found it incomprehensible to turn her baby over to the unknown and wanted to meet the prospective parents. She was pushing her caseworker to break new ground. The agency was a bit wary but respected Phoebe's sincerity and was willing to honor her request. Back then the agency did the decision-making as to which families would receive particular children. Since we apparently were more comfortable with openness than other prospective parents, we were selected for Phoebe's expected child. The plan called for a meeting around the time of birth.

We met on a sunny warm day in May about three weeks before Sara was born. We were nervous and chose our words carefully, realizing that everything we said took on special importance. Gradually we relaxed and began to enjoy this rare and exquisite occasion.

At one point in our meeting, Phoebe's caseworker reminded us that "it takes a little rain and a bit of sunshine to make a rainbow" referring to the loss that Phoebe was experiencing and the joy we were. Little Sara was the rainbow—a beautiful person-to-be that all of us would love and care for.

The impact of this meeting was dramatic. We did not realize it at that time, but that meeting linked us forever as family. Our worlds had grown in a profound manner. As it turned out, the agency also grew as a result of that meeting. Recognizing from our experience that birthparents and adoptive parents are fully capable of respecting and caring for each other, they were emboldened to continue their evolution toward openness as standard practice.

We met Phoebe once again, in the hospital after Sara was born, but after that we exchanged letters and pictures only and did not meet again until Sara was three years old. During the exchange of letters Phoebe once wrote, "I thank God that He chose you to be Sara's parents." It was reassuring to us that she accepted Sara's adoption and that she accepted us.

Our trust continued to grow as we continually were made aware of Phoebe's love for Sara. We, of course, had come to cherish our beautiful little daughter and it seemed natural for us to surround Sara with the people that loved her as well. We invited Phoebe to come visit us in our home so she could meet her daughter again and establish a personal relationship that would continue throughout Sara's life. Sara, a precocious three-year-old, met Phoebe at the door. "Hi, I'm Sara. You must be Phoebe. Come on in. This is my mom. Her name is Julie but everybody calls her Tookie. This is my dad. His name is Ric. And here is my baby sister Laura. She's adopted too! I'll show you my bedroom . . ." Later on as we all sat at the lunch table, Sara turned to me and said, "Mom, did you know that I started in Phoebe's tummy?"

As the years have gone by, Phoebe has remained an important part of our family. While there have been many warm moments, certainly one of the highlights of our relationship was attending her wedding. It was a special day and it only seemed natural that we were there. All of our previous meetings together took place in our home. But now we were invited into Phoebe's world. She wanted a small wedding with just close friends and family. Of course, we felt like honored guests. She introduced us to her family and we were touched by the opportunity to share in this happy occasion.

Phoebe continues to share her love with both of our daughters. We are deeply appreciative of that sensitivity since our second daughter, who is now six years old, has not yet met her birthmother.

Laura has been in touch through letters and pictures but, above all, would love to meet her birthmother. Sometimes she wonders why her birthmother hasn't visited yet since Phoebe has come so often. But Phoebe has filled this void for the time being. She brings presents for both, takes them on special excursions, and simply demonstrates a love and concern for both of them. Sometimes Sara is a little jealous and says, "Laura, remember, she's MY birthmom." At those times we long for Laura's birthmom to join us. She knows she is welcome.

In our daughters' day-to-day lives they have come to understand what it means to have two families, and it is very natural and commonplace. Recently Laura has developed a relationship with her birth great-grandparents. They have sent letters, cards, gifts, and pictures of Laura's birthmother when she was a child. In her bedtime prayers each night Laura says, "God bless Grandma and Grandpa, Grandma and Grandpa, Grandma and Grandpa." One night after she prayed for all three sets of grandparents, she stopped and wondered out loud if there were any more grandparents she needed to include.

Sara often wonders from whom she inherits certain characteristics. She commented one night that she was the most patient person in our family so she must have "gotten her patience from Phoebe." She also has decided she gets her silliness from Ric since he is, in her words, "the craziest dad I know." In Sara's mind open adoption makes sense. This was illustrated clearly one night as we were watching television. It was quickly evident that the program's plot centered on an adoptee who was searching for her birthmother. Sara was astounded by what she saw. "That girl is adopted and she doesn't know her birthmother. That's really weird!"

The question we are most often asked is, "How do you handle open adoption?" as if it is something difficult to cope with. We sense a concern that if our daughters have two sets of parents there is confusion of parental authority. But we are confident in our roles as nuturing parents and know that Phoebe would never undercut our authority with Sara. We also sense that people fear there must be competition for Sara's and Laura's love between the two families. But this simply has not happened. What *has* happened is that love has been doubled, not divided. In the beginning of Sara's relationship with Phoebe, Sara questioned me. "Are you always going to be my mom?" and "Could I ever live with Phoebe?" With reassurances and explanations that I was her mom but that Phoebe would always be a special person in her life, she settled it in her mind that she was, in her words, "lucky to have two moms to love."

The emotional experiences of our initial meetings, our exchange of letters, and our meeting with Phoebe when Sara was three years old have developed into natural experiences where we are more relaxed, more willing to communicate our feelings, and able to see that we share a common vision—the love and welfare of our children. We are very hopeful that soon we will meet for the first time with Laura's birthmother. We know that will be an emotional experience. But we know that what may start in anxiety will surely develop into a comfortable and natural relationship. We will experience the satisfaction of seeing our family grow once more.

Bob and Anita Dombroski

*"They had selected **us**"*

We have a daughter, Kara, age 3½. She was born on February 26, 1984, at a downtown hospital in Grand Rapids. I remember viewing the city from a hospital window. It was cold, heavy, drained of primary color. An old church spire rose among the featureless office buildings. In contrast to the drabness of the city, the sky was a vivid blue. It could have been, I suppose, most any midwestern city.

Anita and I were busy professionals, preoccupied with the dry details and schedules of our office routines. She is a community college administrator and nursing teacher, a gatekeeper to modest hopes of employment and respectability. I am an attorney who, at that time, was swamped by the domestic turbulence the rustic poor women of Northern Michigan washed into my cramped legal aid office. "Blessed are the peacemakers," I would note with irony on the many bad days.

Traverse City is a pleasant place, with the usual problems and small comforts of Middle America. We are surrounded by a graceful beauty of water, orchards, sand hills, and woods, and convinced that we reside in the best of possible worlds. We are blessed and encumbered by our distance apart—at least a full day's automobile ride over secondary roads—from everything else.

A few days earlier, we had traveled with Jim Gritter to Grand Rapids. We met Marlene and Blue in a decrepit, but spotlessly neat, upstairs apartment. Their door lacked a knob. A glimpse of back-yard wrecks of cars and the murmur of neighborhood toughs intruded through the hole; a recognizable odor of natural gas drenched the aged brownish walls. The flotsam of used and borrowed household goods punctured by an orderly tower of massive electronic amplifiers and the other tools of a performing band surrounded us. Jim acted as an intermediary: the timeless interpreter of one tribe's folkways to supplicants from a distant tribe. The light nervousness and self-consciousness of the guest in the strange home was imposed upon the hesitant modesty of a young, poor, and very pregnant girl.

The drift of the conversation will forever be lost; one large fact dominated us all. Marlene and Blue had selected us, from a file folder of forms, to be the parents of their child. Even now, this memory overwhelms the course of what is happening. We found we liked each other, and made our plans together.

Not surprisingly, neither Anita nor I are natives of Traverse City and we both believe it will not be in our best career interests to long remain here. She is the farm daughter of a Michigan schoolteacher. Like many Midwestern youth who leave the farm, she is talented, well-read, and of fierce, independent political intellect. I am the product of mid-century Connecticut: a very comfortable lower-middle-class childhood, well-educated by parents who equated formal education with opportunity and who dutifully paid homage to the status-conscious values of the WASP elite that still define East Coast culture and respectability. Notwithstanding those differences, we share one great common denominator of the legendary Fifties: Catholic parochial elementary school. In other words, nothing in either of our backgrounds prepared us for what was to happen.

A few days later we were visiting friends in Muskegon. While taking in an evening movie (Woody Allen's *Broadway Danny Rose*), we were paged by an usher and told that Marlene had called from Grand Rapids. We knew she was in labor and we arrived at the hospital one hour later.

The process which we had been through began years ago with

the grudging and never fully realized acceptance of the fact that we would never naturally conceive and give birth to a child. Measure by measure—from clinic to counseling, from reading the available literature to talking among friends—our options ran down as we drifted through time. We found ourselves well into our thirties and childless. Sometime in this course of events, we had placed our names with the two available local adoption agencies. One, we were told, was "traditional"; the other dealt in "open adoption." As the waiting list stretched on for years, I assigned no significance to these labels, other than the notion that the word "open" (as in "open marriage" or "open city") connoted something both progressive and, perhaps, disreputable.

One day a letter affixed with the reassuring but intimidating cross and coat of arms of the local Catholic diocese awaited. A meeting beckoned at the office of the agency, an antiseptically cheerful modern building, half hidden in a row of state administrative and social service agency branch office buildings. In a white-lit classroom, a large circle of uncomfortable looking couples in uncomfortable chairs stared at us as we entered. We were now among the marked, I felt, and summoned up all the protective devices of the middle class when confronted with a strange and possibly socially threatening group situation. "How should we behave?" was the pregnant question etched on each anxious face.

A young, slightly unkempt social worker carried forward an introductory explanation and a dry description of the timetable and costs. Although memory, in part, fails, I recall that at an early point the polite demand was made to each person to make a statement; this produced a palpable mental scramble to verbally present oneself in an appropriate manner. Caution was, of course, the unspoken watchword. We were coached by old friends (who had years earlier gone through an adoption elsewhere) to imagine ourselves as a non-controversial Catholic couple and express ourselves accordingly in order to avoid difficulty. In due course, the irrepressible desire to redefine ourselves and our motives overcame these barriers, and we all rediscovered ourselves as a decent bunch of friends and neighbors.

Meetings progressed. The most startling facet of open

adoption was the principle of reverse selectivity. We of the middle class are accustomed to being in direct control of things, or delegating that control to our institutions (adoption agencies, in this case), which we trust as dependable custodians of our social power. We didn't yet fully appreciate the full impact of what was going to happen to us: We were going to be selected by birthparents rather than directly controlling the selection of our future children ourselves or delegating that control to the agency. There was no list or picturebook of deprived children awaiting our benevolence, no go-between acting primarily as our agent. Quickly, Jim, the agency worker, made it clear that he was far more concerned with the birthmother's freedom of choice than ours. Although we kidded ourselves that, after all, Jim was "one of us", we increasingly were aware that we were on the outside looking in, as prospective birthmothers and -fathers planned their futures with Jim or Abbie, the other agency worker.

Of course, this is but one dimension of our experience, which led toward mutual trust, respect, and love. But it is most noteworthy, because it most reverses the accepted way things work in our culture.

Incidentally, although some of us waited longer while a few couples joyfully received children from birthparents, we all experienced this same unique experience of parenthood with our new friends as each couple in the end was selected. The resentfulness of being chosen "last" while others had "their" children finally passed as we were caught up in the excitement of our long-awaited special experience.

Marlene had a healthy baby girl and named her Kara. Anita assisted in the delivery. For the next three days Marlene, Blue, Anita, Marlene's family, and I felt the emotional ups and downs that this suddenly-present baby girl in the maternity ward nursery conjured up in each of us. "How is each of us to accept her?" I thought as I watched her. I remember giving Kara her first bath, feeling conscious of my clumsiness as the ward nurse, with amused tolerance and much coaching, helped me along. Throughout, Marlene struggled with the decision to give Kara up to us, while we struggled helplessly with the possibility that she would decide

to keep Kara to raise as her own daughter. While this inner turmoil affected our communication with each other, it created a bond
around Kara that she would always know was her special destiny,
and that we all would value highly.

On a cold Thursday afternoon, after four days in the hosptial,
we all left. By the main entrance, Marlene gave Kara to us as we
all stood dwarfed by the building above and the traffic in front.
We carefully placed Kara in her restraint seat between us and drove
off north to her new home. It was a tearful, heart-rending moment,
as difficult to re-express as it was initially to express to each other.
It overwhelmed each of us.

Marlene and Blue, after formally releasing Kara to us in a Probate Court proceeding four months after her birth, have pursued
their young destinies with jobs, moves, and finally marriages, each
with someone new and special in their lives. Although we maintain contact with less frequency as time passes, we find we enjoy
getting together, even if only by letter or telephone call, to share
some new development or discovery Kara has experienced as she
grows. There is much to report about Kara since she has developed into a running, jumping, talking, all-around American kid,
and Marlene and Blue are always delighted listeners. They fully
understand that they will always be welcome members of our family.

Mike and Jean Spry—I

"An extraordinary moment"

Bob and Anita had lost their minds. It was the only logical explanation for what they were doing. After years of frustration, had
their desire to adopt a baby turned to desperation? It wasn't difficult
to share their enthusiasm; the prospect of finally being able to
adopt an infant in the not-too-distant future was definitely exciting. It was the rest of the scenario that was hard to believe.

It was at least peculiar that they would be selected for the adoptive placement, not by someone professionally trained in such
decision-making, but *by the mother of the baby*, who would pick
them out from a group of portfolios on available adoptive couples.
Then, she might actually decide to *meet them* before finalizing
her decision. How could the agency possibly hope to prevent the
disclosure of identifying information with such an approach? In
fact, the agency had no intention of assuring secrecy and actually
encouraged the biological parents (both mother and father) to establish an *ongoing relationship* with the adoptive parents and the
adopted child. This was scandalous! Who could have conceived
of such an idea? What would prevent a "birth" mother or father
from later absconding with their child if they knew where to find
it? Wouldn't it be awfully irritating for the adoptive parents to have
the birthparents continually underfoot, perhaps interfering with
their approach to child-rearing? Wouldn't the adoptive parents be
concerned that their own bond with the child would be undermined

by the presence of the *real* parents? How could Bob and Anita consider exposing themselves to such incredible risks and impositions?

There was more. After being selected by the mother prior to the birth of the child, Bob and Anita would be faced with the possibility that she might *change her mind* and keep the baby! In fact, she could regain custody of the child up to eight weeks after the baby was placed in their home. In other words, they could spend two months bonding with their baby, falling more in love with it everyday, only to be heartbroken by having the child suddenly torn from their lives. How could any reasonable person ask Bob and Anita to take such a potentially devastating risk? How could they even consider accepting such a risk? It was unfathomable! They had definitely gone crazy.

Over two years later, we still try to keep these reactions fresh in our minds; it makes it much easier to accept similar verbalizations from other people when we explain our own "open adoption." We have to remember that neither of us had much acceptance or understanding for the concept the first time we heard about it. It is important that we recall that it took several months for us to come to grips with our misconceptions and that we can't expect everyone else to embrace the idea in a matter of minutes. Alas, many of us fall victim to the traps of traditional adoptive thinking and come to think that the traditional form of adoption is the only sensible way to proceed, as though it was handed down on stone tablets. Much of the story of openness in adoption, therefore, is about the transformation in thinking for many adoptive couples—the process that turns them from skeptics to virtual disciples of the program.

For us the change came slowly. As Bob and Anita went through the orientation and education phase, the home study, and ultimately awaited the placement of their baby, we learned a lot from them. We discovered that the birthparents (usually just the birthmother) make no attempt to serve as co-parents or interfere with the adoptive family, but rather take on the role of a 'special friend'—like a doting aunt, uncle, cousin, or older sibling. After all, birthparents release a baby for adoption to try to give it the best possible start in life; they want to *enhance* the child's family life, not *disrupt* it. We also began to acknowledge the fact that the secrecy in traditional adoption was problematic for many adoptees. We both knew adoptees who were troubled by their lack of knowledge about their genetic and familial heritage; these people had diligently searched for their birthparents as though they could not feel whole without satisfying that need. Perhaps having the birthparents around to solve many of the mysteries wasn't such a bad idea.

An event that had enormous impact on our thinking was the birth of Bob and Anita's adoptive daughter, Kara. The fact that they were able to be at the hospital for the birth was profound; the fact that Anita was actually able to *participate in the delivery* was awe-inspiring. Imagine an adoptive mother being present at that magic moment when her baby takes its first breath! Then, both Bob and Anita were able to spend time with the baby in the hospital. When the day came for Kara to be released from the hospital, there was no six-week stay for the baby in foster care; Bob and Anita took her home. What adoptive parent wouldn't walk through fire for such an opportunity?

Yes, Bob and Anita still faced the real possibility that their birthmother would reverse her decision, and they undoubtedly felt more than a little fearful during those early weeks. Clearly, however, we had misplaced our concerns about the risks entailed during this time—we had narrowly focused on the potential for loss and emotional pain without acknowledging a far greater potential for good outcomes. As a prospective adoptive parent, if you were offered the chance to take your baby home from the hospital, and perhaps (with the consent of the birthmother) be on hand for the birth, you would naturally be interested. In this program, the price for this opportunity is risk—risking that you might have to absorb a significant loss, confer your blessing on a birthparent who has struggled with an extraordinarily difficult decision, and then wait for another birthparent to select you. (In about ten percent of the placements from the hospital, this risk becomes reality.) For some people, this price might seem too high; to us the potential benefits clearly outweighed the risks. To be able to bond with your adopted baby from the very start and to have some chance of being present at the birth seemed well worth a walk through emotional fire.

By the time we gave up on our own fertility and decided to proceed with plans for adoption, we had become convinced that we wanted an open arrangement. When we went to our first orientation session, we had to bridle our impatience, thinking that we had little more to learn about the concept. Once again, we were wrong. The orientation and education sessions certainly gave us confidence that we had made the right decision, but they also forced us to re-examine our thinking about every single aspect of adoption.

Particularly influential at this time was our reading of Betty Jean Lifton's *Lost and Found*—a book that had been recommended by the agency's child welfare supervisor, Jim Gritter. If there ever was a blatant indictment of the problems inherent in traditional adoption, this is it. Even granting that the tone of the book may be colored by the author's own experience as an adoptee, it is a work to be reckoned with and will challenge virtually every notion about adoption one has ever entertained. (For the person considering adoption as an avenue to parenthood, the book can get more than a little depressing at times; the reader might want to skip ahead to the section on openness if feelings of hopelessness start to set in.) Far more than any other single source, this book helped us to see the special needs of all those affected by adoption—the birthparents, the adoptive parents, the extended families, and especially the adoptee.

Reading *Lost and Found* also eradicated the one last fear that we harbored about openness—that our adopted child's ongoing relationship with a birthparent might in some way lesson the strength and intensity of our own bond. In writing her book, Ms. Lifton interviewed a number of adult adoptees who had searched for and found their biological parents. An almost universal response was that the acquaintance with their birthparents had only made them feel *closer* to their adoptive parents, especially when the adoptive parents had assisted in the search. Many reported that, because they could finally get in touch with their genetic heritage, they had a far better sense of the relative contribution made by their adoptive parents to their development and identity. This significantly heightened their appreciation for the relationship with their adoptive parents. Reading these accounts, we became convinced that there was nothing to lose in having ongoing contact with a birthparent; our relationship with our adopted child would probably be better and stronger, and the child would have a more integrated sense of identity.

After all of the group discussions at the agency and all of the reading we had done, and by the time we completed the home study (and the mountains of paperwork that went along with it), we were four-square behind the concept of openness in adoption. Only two fears remained: 1) that we might be one of the couples who would be selected only to see the birthmother change her mind, and 2) that the birthparents who selected us would *not* want an open relationship.

Next came the waiting phase, which also differs from what is seen in traditional adoption. In traditional adoption, after you are approved by the agency, you go on a list and wait until your name reaches the top. Often the waiting period lasts several years. Because the birthparents make the selections in this program, you could be chosen at any time after successful completion of the home study. In fact, the agency cautions couples to inform them of any out-of-town travel plans and to be ready to spring into action at a moment's notice because some of the placements come together suddenly. In our group of prospective adoptive parents, a grapevine evolved to share any news gleaned about upcoming placements so that we might better foresee getting "the call." During some weeks, it seemed like everytime the phone rang, anticipation would well up and we would wonder, "Is this it?" At other times we got despondent and pessimistic. After a while, we just tried to keep the whole thing out of our minds. Of course, when "the call" finally came, it was when we least expected it.

On a Friday in January of 1985 at 4:45 P.M., at a time when most people are wasting away the final minutes of the work week, the phone rang. It was Abbie Nelson, the agency's pregnancy counselor. She said that there was a young woman in her office who would be giving birth in about three to four weeks and wanted to release her baby to us; she also wanted to schedule a time when we all could meet. We made an appointment to meet the following Tuesday and then we celebrated!

Skyrockets were igniting in our imaginations! It is hard to adequately describe the wild excitement we felt at the time. Perhaps the old cliché, "it was like Christmas and the Fourth of July all rolled into one" is apt. The only thing tempering our emotions was the knowledge that the situation could reverse itself suddenly, but we did not let that bother us very much. Months earlier we had decided that, once selected, we would proceed optimistically and try to thoroughly enjoy every anticipatory moment. We felt that if the birthmother changed her mind, we would be able to pick up the pieces and go on. For now, we were quite content to let our hearts fly.

We drove to our Tuesday night meeting filled with all sorts of questions and conflicting emotions—eagerness, apprehension, confidence, and doubt. Would she like us? Would we like her? Would she want an open relationship? Would she let us be at the hospital for the birth? How could we make her more comfortable with her choice? Our minds were racing.

Occasionally in life, people have the rare opportunity to find themselves participating in a profoundly moving human experience. The night we met our birthmother, Reneé, and her mother, Penny, was one of those times. Simple words are not sufficient to describe what happened in that room. At first, everyone seemed a little tense. They seemed to be as concerned about our liking them as we were about them liking us. Soon the ice was broken, however, and we began to get better acquainted and make plans for the upcoming birth. We were instantly impressed with them; Reneé was pretty, intelligent, and personable; Penny was warm, friendly, and very supportive of her daughter.

Reneé said that she wanted us at the hospital for the birth (but not in the delivery room) and wanted to see us interact with the baby. She emphatically stated that she would take care of her baby in the hospital and we let her know that, as far as we were concerned, she would be "in charge" there. We discussed our willingness to have an open relationship, but Reneé informed us that she only wanted to exchange letters and pictures, she did not want to have face-to-face contact. We told her that we would honor her wishes, but we would be comfortable with renegotiating our relationship if she later desired more openness. We talked about names and decided that we would all try to name the baby together in the hospital. We discussed child-care plans, extended families, the birthfather (who was denying paternity), Reneé's studies at school, how we planned to explain the adoption to the child, and many other things.

All too quickly, our meeting was over. We all hugged each other, and the two of us adjourned to the lobby with Penny while Reneé met with Abbie. There we talked some more and told Penny how delighted we were to have been picked by Reneé. We were surprised and saddened to find that Penny need reassurance from us; she was concerned that we know that Reneé was "a good girl." We told her that we had no doubts about that. She then looked at us with tears in her eyes and said, "Ever since Reneé told me she was pregnant, I have asked myself over and over again why this had to happen; I guess maybe you're the reason."

The week before the birth was a veritable whirlwind of activity—the beginning of labor symptoms on Sunday, visiting Reneé's home and meeting the rest of her family, rushing to the hospital at 3 A.M. ("false labor"), attending a childbirth class with Reneé and Penny, doctor appointments, and lots of phone calls. Reneé and her family really went out of their way to include us in the anticipatory events. Every morning we would wake up and think, "This will be the day," and every night we went to bed thinking that certainly tomorrow would be.

Finally, it was decided that a Caesarean delivery would be necessary and a Friday appointment was set with the physician who would be doing it. We thought that he would certainly admit Reneé to the hospital immediately after the examination and that Friday would be "the day." We woke up that morning all ready to go, only to have the doctor schedule the C-section for the following Tuesday. After getting all psyched-up, this was quite a disappointment. We soon regained our perspective, though, and resolved that we would spend the next few days taking care of loose ends and going out for one last fling together. It was at least comforting to finally know when the baby would be born, and we prepared for a relaxing weekend.

The baby, already showing signs of independent judgement, had quite another set of plans. On Saturday morning at 4 A.M. we got a call from Penny at the hospital. Reneé had gone into labor and an emergency C-section was being quickly arranged. We threw ourselves into our clothes and set a new course record for the 18-mile jaunt into Traverse City. We raced up the stairs to the maternity ward and immediately ran into Penny and her husband Tom (Reneé's step-father) who filled us in on the pertinent details, Penny told us that, while Reneé definitely wanted us to be with the baby after the delivery, she also wished to be the first one to *hold* the baby. We knew it would be hard to resist temptation, but we agreed to honor her request. Reneé was taken to the operating room at 5 A.M. as the four of us filed into the "Stork Club" for some anxious nail-biting.

At about 5:25 A.M., Dr. Smith carried a little bundle into the room and asked that we all follow him to the nursery. We each scrubbed up and watched in awe as he placed a beautiful baby girl down under the light. What an extraordinary moment! We looked at her in utter disbelief; could this gorgeous child be the one who would become our adopted daughter? It was love at first sight—at least for the four adults who were studying her intently; the baby was rather preoccupied with loud protests of her rude treatment in this strange new world. We were literally mesmerized as we gently stroked this precious child. Whatever risks we were taking by being here were certainly well worth the experience! How many adoptive parents get a change to give their baby its first bath in the nursery? Luckily, we did, although we had to ask the nurse to pick her up at one point so that Reneé would be the first one of us to hold her. What an amazing and unforgettable time it was.

After Reneé was wheeled up from the recovery room and we all had a chance to hold the baby, we went down to her room and found (to our surprise) that she was ready to talk about naming her baby. The first name that came up was 'Lara'—one we had discussed in our very first meeting. The three of us thought that it was a good name for such a beautiful little girl, so 'Lara' it was. Then we asked Reneé how she would feel about giving the baby

'Reneé' as a middle name. There was quick agreement. Thus, the three of us named the baby 'Lara Reneé.'

The next few days were wonderful. Reneé allowed us ample opportunities to be alone with the baby so we could bond as we fed, diapered, and held her. We also spent time talking with Reneé. She really seemed to enjoy seeing us with Lara.

Things began to change, however, about halfway into the hospital stay. Our adoption worker had warned us that this was common in Caesarean births—that when the birthmother regains her strength, she takes a more active interest in her baby. In the agency's experience, they had seen some of these birthmothers change their minds about releasing. We started to pick up some negative vibrations from Reneé and began to tread carefully in our dealings with her. She asked that we stay away from the hospital for one day while she cared for Lara. We certainly understood her need for this and graciously complied, but while we sat at home we wondered what was going through her mind and feared that she might reverse her decision. We were mentally prepared to back out if we had to.

On the night before Lara's scheduled discharge, we went back up to the hospital to talk with Reneé and Penny. Reneé seemed angry and almost resentful when we held the baby. We knew that something wasn't right. We then talked with Penny alone and she confirmed our suspicion that Reneé had been considering ways to keep her baby. We told Penny that we were prepared to gracefully bow out if Reneé decided not to release. Penny, however, had been counseling Reneé to follow through with her original plan. They would be discussing it further over dinner.

When they returned from dinner, we were told that Reneé had decided to release Lara to us, although she clearly had some reservations about her decision. Reneé instructed us to bring a baby outfit and an infant car seat for the discharge on the following morning. We reminded her that we were quite comfortable with having a more open relationship if she wanted that. She told us that both she and her mother had decided that they, too, wanted openness. While we were glad that Reneé had decided to release and that she wanted ongoing contact, we left the hospital more than a little tense. We knew that anything could happen, even yet.

The next morning we discussed the situation with Abbie Nelson. She told us that the discharge was scheduled for 11 A.M. and that Reneé had insisted that the baby be discharged to her. The hospital, therefore would not allow us to take the baby from Reneé in the building. Abbie had arranged it so that, after exiting the hospital, Reneé would place Lara in our car and then leave. We were to bring up the clothes and car seat, then wait in the lobby.

You would expect that when adoptive parents finally get their baby, they would be filled with joy. This was hardly the case. We followed Abbie's instructions to the letter and waited for Reneé, Penny, and Lara. When we saw them coming, we went out to the car to see one of the most heartrending scenes you could imagine. Crying, Reneé put Lara in our vehicle, closed the door, and walked to her car. We wanted to say something to her, but she clearly did not want to talk to us. Crying, we each hugged Penny. "Take good care of her," she said.

Some people have asked us how we could possibly put ourselves through that experience. Frankly, as emotionally painful as it was, we are glad that we were there. We will always know that the source of our joy was a birthmother who faced the most difficult decision of her life, and who had the courage and love to endure a most painful moment so that her daughter could have the best possible start in life. Our sense of gratitude to this young woman who chose *us* to raise her child, is so much more intense and heartfelt because we were there at the time of release. Someday, when Lara asks if Reneé loved her, we can tell her with conviction, authority, and vivid memories that Reneé loved her very, very much.

Over seventeen months have passed since we brought Lara home from the hospital and it now seems hard to conceive that we ever had even the slightest objections to openness in adoption. Frankly, after all we went through and with the gratitude we felt toward Reneé, it would have been very difficult to see her simply walk out of our lives forever. We are thankful that she chose openness. Reneé made her first visit to our home just over a week after the release. She already seemed to be much more comfortable with her decision. Since then, we have talked on the phone or face-to-face on the average of about once a month. We pretty much let Reneé set the pace for the frequency of contact based on her degree of desire and comfort.

We have had a number of very meaningful encounters with Reneé and her family. One of the most touching was attending her high school graduation and open house. There we met many members of her extended family—aunts, uncles, cousins, etc.—as well as a number of her friends. Nearly everyone greeted us warmly and enthusiastically. Seeing the baby obviously meant a lot to many of the family members; it felt good to be able to share Lara with them. It was also nice to see Reneé take pride in Lara as she showed her to friends and family; her degree of openness, honesty, and acceptance in dealing with the adoption seemed amazingly healthy.

Just before Christmas, we got together with Reneé, her brother and sister, and Penny. Lara had just started walking and it was great to see everyone enjoying this stage of her development. Reneé gave Lara a stuffed Winnie the Pooh bear which remains one of her favorite toys. Just before leaving, we had a round of hugs and Penny said to us, "Thank you for taking such good care of her, I knew you would." It felt so warm and comforting to hear those words.

For Lara's first birthday, we had a celebration with family on hand for dinner and cake. Early in the afternoon, Reneé called and we invited her and her new boyfriend to share in the festivities. This marked the first time she had ever met any of our extended family and it went extremely well. Many of our family members also feel a sense of gratitude to the young woman who made our dreams a reality, and they finally got a chance to express it. It was a very special and memorable day.

Our relationship with Reneé and her family continues to evolve and is very rewarding. Perhaps the infrequency of contact has been one of the biggest surprises. We can only speculate that when a birthmother can see her child very readily—in our case simply by calling to see if it's convenient—the need to actually make contact becomes less compelling. Regardless, we are looking forward to having Reneé be a special part of our family for years to come.

Kathy and Mike Kundrat

"A special friend in Katie's life"

As my new friend Jean and I—both childless—sat commiserating over a plate of nachos at the local Mexican restaurant, I realized that one of the most absolutely wonderful things about the open adoption program was being part of a group. Jean Spry and I and our husbands, both named Mike, had started the program together on a hot day in August. We were introduced to the concept together; we had struggled through the paperwork and the interviews together. We met for dinner and speculated on birthmoms together. We windowshopped for baby clothes and discussed which cribs were best together. We were "expectant" couples sharing the same dreams and fears. All through the fall we waited and talked and called and wondered. Rumors were rampant, and we loved it. Any news was good news because it was something to share.

The agency had encouraged us to get to know each other, and our group of eight couples seemed eager to meet and discuss our mutual feelings. We met at each other's houses, sometimes with Jim Gritter—more often on our own. We came from diverse backgrounds but it was pleasant to be with people who shared feelings of loss connected to infertility and the impatience associated with adoption. The meetings became the high point of our social calendars as we waited together.

This connection brought Jean and me to the Mexican restaurant because it was a cold, blustery day in January, and we needed to reassure ourselves that the dreams that began in August were really going to happen. That day is vivid to me because I realized that we had become friends, and we weren't talking only of rumors and babies but about us as people. Two couples in the group had been chosen, so we knew that dreams could become reality. We just had to wait until a birthmom decided we were the ones for her. So we left each other with plans for diet and exercise until our big day arrived. That night Jean called and said she and Mike had been chosen! Abbie had called from the agency and the baby was due very soon. We were *so* excited; Mike and I felt such happiness for our new friends. It was as if we could reach out and touch their joy. We eagerly shared their experience over the next month—Lara's birth, homecoming, and settling in. Their happiness filled the gap as we continued to wait . . .

On March 9 the group was scheduled to meet at our house. Mike and I spent all day cleaning and cooking, hoping to provide a pleasant evening for everyone. Mike even made pasta from scratch to go with the spaghetti sauce, and the garlic bread filled the house with a great aroma. Lara and Lauren, the new additions to the group, were coming too, so we stoked up the wood to be sure it was nice and warm. (Lauren had been placed with Mike and Mary, who, along with Mike and Jean, and Mike and me, became something of a subgroup which we kiddingly called the "Mikes and Moms Club.")

Everyone arrived; we drank some wine and cuddled the babies. Those of us not yet chosen cheered each other up with the latest rumors. The pasta had just begun to boil when the phone rang. I left the room to answer it. It was Abbie! She said if we weren't doing anything the next day that maybe we would like to come to the hospital and meet our new baby girl!

Jean walked by, and when I said, "It's Abbie", she ran to get Mike. As Mike and I listened to Teresa's story, we both stood very still. I can remember trying to be calm and rational—still trying to say the right things to Abbie. Truthfully, my mind was filled with such fear and excitement that I could hardly breathe, let alone talk.

As we hung up, I could smell the homemade pasta burning, and I could hear the smoke alarm's shrill sound. So what! Nothing mattered. It was a perfect moment. Total empathy and excitement filled the room.

We threw the smoke alarm out into the snow and began to share the news that Abbie had given us. Teresa wanted to release to us; however, her aunt and uncle were at the hospital. They were considering adopting the baby. Teresa would be meeting with them to let them know her plans concerning us. Abbie cautioned that plans could change during this kind of meeting and that she would call us in a little while—as soon as she knew.

So here we were, with a pot of spaghetti and people we had come to know so well, waiting again. As we ate dinner we talked about all the things we needed to get ready. We had set up a nursery, but the little, most important, things we still needed to buy—like diapers! And, of course, something pink! We had anticipated meeting our birth mom prior to the birth, so we would have more time to prepare. However, at this point, preparation time was furthest from our minds. This small-talk filled dinner time, something to do—while we waited . . .

It was 9:15 and still no call. I was being totally pessimistic about the outcome while Mike tried to reassure me that time was all we needed. The group sat around going through the alphabet—coming up with outrageous names for the little girl we hoped would be ours. Needless to say, none of their suggestions supplanted the name we preferred, which was Katie.

At 11:00—still no call, and I can still picture people starting to nod off on the couch. The phone rang—we answered together, and Abbie's voice said no firm decision had been made, but it looked pretty good for us. She'd call first thing in the morning to let us know whether or not to come. No one wanted to leave, but they had to. So with hugs and tears we said good-bye and promised to let them know as soon as we heard.

Mike can sleep in a rock concert, so he went to bed, and I lay staring at the darkness waiting for morning . . .

At 9:30 Abbie called and said, "Come to the hospital at 11:00 and meet your baby." Anxiety and happiness is not a common mix of emotions but that's what we felt. I tried to call my folks, but no answer. Now that we could share our news, I wanted to tell everyone.

During the 30-minute ride to the hospital, we were quiet, both thinking our own thoughts. What I now realize about that ride is that it was our last act as a couple—since that day we have been a family. What carefree days couples can have! Once you are a parent, you are never as carefree again, but if you're ready for it, the trade-off is worth it.

As we hurried toward the elevator, carrying a diaper bag(!), we recalled how often we had visited here to welcome new babies of close friends. Now it was actually happening to us.

The heat from the maternity ward seemed suffocating as we opened the door. There was Abbie at the very end of the long hall. She pointed behind us, we turned, and there was Teresa smiling the best smile we had ever seen. We walked together toward her room, and as we passed the viewing area, my eyes scanned all the babies. Where was she? In Teresa's room we talked, and I showed her some of the things we'd brought for the baby. We shared our feelings of inadequacy to care for such a tiny being. Finally, Abbie said we could come to meet the baby. They dressed us in hospital gowns and took us into a room with a rocking chair. In came a nurse holding what we were sure was the world's most perfect baby. It was feeding time, and she gave me a bottle to give her. As I held her and fed her, Mike and Teresa sat watching. Occasionally, Teresa would reach over and touch the baby's hand or head.

At this point, Abbie tactfully suggested that we leave while Teresa said her farewells to the baby. We told the nurses we would be back in one hour, and we hurried to a supermarket to fill a cart with necessities. I finally reached my folks, and they planned to meet us at the hospital.

Back at the hospital, the nurses showed us how to bathe the baby. They had picked out what she should wear home and said I could dress her. Me? How could I dress such a tiny, delicate person? Surprisingly, Katie was very cooperative. She just stared at me with those beautiful eyes I would soon know so well.

Waiting in the hall were not only my Mom and Dad but two aunts and an uncle. Everyone was crying and hugging. I was so happy to have this moment to share with the people who had nurtured me for so long. Needless to say, the nurses were impressed, and I've heard they still talk about the tribe that picked up one little baby.

The next month was a whirlwind—showers, letters, cards, phone calls, sleepless nights, and peanut butter sandwiches. No more homemade pasta for a while! Of course, best of all was Katie. As we learned to love each other, I was constantly amazed at the depth of feeling that could be elicited by a child.

We had been so prepared for openness in our adoption that we were very disappointed that we hadn't heard anything from Teresa since we had met her in the hospital. The court date passed without a hitch. We were almost beginning to believe our well-meaning friends and relatives when they said things like, "It's better this way" or "You don't want any trouble." It was difficult to pinpoint what we were feeling. We were so happy to be a family, and yet we really wanted that other piece that we had anticipated—contact with Teresa.

Well, one November day it happened. Abbie called and said Teresa would like to visit Katie. Talk about bells going off! Why did she want to see her now—after six months? What did this mean? Here we were alarmed over something we'd been wishing would happen. We arranged to meet at the agency. We dressed Katie in her cutest clothes (we wanted Teresa to be assured that she had made the right choice) and drove slowly into town.

We settled in an office with Teresa and Katie's birthfather's sister Susie. Katie sat on the floor being beautiful and giving us all a focal point for conversation. Teresa gave Katie a sweet little teddy bear, and when Katie hugged it, we could tell that Teresa was happy. Fortunately, they had brought their camera along and were able to capture many wonderful moments. We were all excited to review pictures from the hospital, and we gave them some to take with them. When it was time to leave, I told Katie to say "bye." She waved bye-bye. Teresa was thrilled. So were we—it was the very first time she'd ever waved bye.

It's hard to believe that Katie will be two in just a few months. Our relationship with Teresa has remained warm and very casual. She is working at a local retail store, and we drop in when we're in town. She called Katie on her first birthday and me on Mother's

Day (I was honored!). I think all of us are comfortable with this relationship. As Katie grows, we hope to keep in contact so that Teresa becomes a special friend in Katie's life. Mike and I are so satisfied with this adoption process and with being parents that it's impossible to believe that our hopes for the future won't be realized.

Prior to becoming parents Mike and I both worked in helping professions. We derived great satisfaction from our work, and we still do. However, that zeal for work has been replaced by a new sense of priorities. Family life is now very crucial. We find ourselves planning family activities first, with other activities a distant second. The joy Katie can bring to a Sunday afternoon is a delightful new experience. As she lets us see her world through her eyes, we can sometimes almost feel her sense of wonder as she learns to be a person. Although she doesn't know it, Katie has helped us through a totally unexpected pregnancy and miscarriage and the sudden death of Mike's father during the past year. Without Katie, it would have been much harder for us to deal with these events. I'm sure most new parents feel these emotions, but the best part is that they seem unique to each individual.

Our original adoption group has gone the way of most groups—we're back to leading our own lives. The "Mikes and Moms" club, though, gets together periodically to share stories and enjoy each other's company. What's even better is that our children (three girls born one month apart) are becoming friends. Our hope is that as the more difficult issues of adoption begin to arise for the girls, they will be close friends and be able to share their thoughts with each other. In addition, they will know that they are not unique or alone — that many children are adopted. We hope that our children will not have to experience the sort of aggravations which historically have frustrated other children denied their birth heritages by means of closed adoption.

We are very thankful to the wise folks who conceived this idea of open adoption. In some ways we feel like pioneers as we attempt to cover new ground and explain the process to those who simply cannot believe that something like this could work.

Recently, I spoke with a colleague who has adopted two children from Korea. During earlier conversations, she was adamantly opposed to openness in adoption. She couldn't imagine knowing the biological parents and thought she would feel threatened by that kind of contact. Well, shortly after her second adoption, she became pregnant. After her baby was born, she began to realize what it would be like to not know where her child was if she had had to give it up. She says that now that she has had the experience of giving birth, she knows that there are two women in Korea who will always wonder what happened to their little girls, and she'll always regret her inability to assure them that their children are safe and that they did a wonderful service by giving them up. Stories like these reassure us that this process is the right choice.

Of course, underneath it all is the fact that whenever Katie reaches a new developmental milestone or hugs me tight and says "Hi, Mommy," I realize that parenting is chemistry, not biology, and I am so happy I was given the opportunity to share my life with a child.

Mary and Mike Vander Kolk

"That crazy 'open adoption' outfit"

Mike and I met in college and got married three years later between his second and third years in medical school. During those first two years I was working 40 hours per week as an intensive care unit nurse and going to school full-time to complete my master's degree in primary care nursing. Our schedules left little time to ourselves, let alone anything else. We both agreed that this was not the best time to start a family. After Mike began his residency and I completed graduate school we started to think about having a "houseful of kids."

When I first learned I was pregnant early in 1980 we were both ecstatic. We told everyone we knew right away. We were equally depressed when I lost the baby two months later. When I became pregnant again that same year, we decided to be more cautious and agreed to wait three months before we "told the world." That caution lasted about two hours—we again were so excited that we started telling all of our friends. By this time, we were seeing an infertility specialist and reasoned that one miscarriage was not uncommon and modern medicine surely had the means to promote healthy pregnancies. But this second pregnancy also ended in a miscarriage.

I was really depressed after that second loss but, being basically optimistic, we continued to hope and try for a healthy baby. Over the next several years, we went through numerous tests, medications, and treatments. On the very day we moved to Traverse City, we tried one last treatment.

That move to Traverse City in June of 1984 was to become the beginning of more than one phase of our lives together. At the age of 32, Mike was finally finished with residency and going into practice "for real." And not just *any* practice—he felt he had managed to secure a position with the best group of general surgeons in the perfect town. He had grown up in a small town in mid-Michigan and had always wanted to end up in a similar place in the northern part of the state. I had spent summers near Traverse City when I was growing up and we had both skiied in that area during the winter months. Both of us enjoyed the seasonal changes and the recreation this area afforded. There was a good-sized hospital were we could both work and a college which offered a nursing program. After graduate school I had taught nursing and hoped to continue that career. In short, Traverse City was exactly what we were looking forward to.

One thing Traverse City did *not* have to offer was a specialist in infertility and the type of care that was available where we previously lived. Our specialist was now 250 miles away; another doctor in that field was three hours away in another direction. Our decision was really not so difficult—we both wanted children and we simply did not have the time to make the frequent long drives that continued treatment would require. Almost as soon as I realized the last treatment was unsuccessful, I called the adoption agencies in our new town.

There were three agencies in the phone book. One specialized in foreign children. One did something called "open adoption." And the third was a traditional agency. I requested information from all three and we prepared to wait the several months until the next informational meeting scheduled at the traditional agency.

In the meantime, we began to hear a lot about that "crazy open adoption outfit across town." We heard stories about how birthparents actually knew where their babies were placed and often maintained a relationship with that child. The stories, of course, were all told by people who knew someone who knew someone else who had heard about this from a friend or neighbor. And they were all told in an incredulous tone of voice, with the additional comment of "just be sure you don't get mixed up in *that!*" Foreign children were not ruled out but they were not our first choice at the time, so that left just one agency.

A few weeks later I was pleasantly surprised to receive a letter about an informational meeting scheduled that same month. We quickly sent in our reply. We knew that traditional adoption would take several years, but we thought we were on our way!

We went to that first meeting with a mixture of excitement and trepidation. Would they actually approve us as potential adoptive parents? How long would we really have to wait for a baby? What is it really like to adopt a baby? But the main thing was that we could continue to hope for a *baby*. We sat down and looked around at the other couples. Everyone was sitting close and holding hands. Jim, the adoption counselor, entered the room and began the meeting by having all of us introduce ourselves. The room seemed to be filled with loving couples who desperately wanted a baby. Would we measure up to the picture these other people presented? Would we meet the expectations for the ideal family into which the agency might choose to place a child?

Then Jim began to explain open adoption. My first thought was surprise that he would talk about the other agency's policies. But as he went on, it was clear that we were *at* that "open adoption outfit." Mike and I looked at each other as we realized what we had done. The two agencies here have somewhat similar names. Apparently, the people who had been scaring us about open adoption didn't even know which agency they were talking about. And in our excitement about starting the adoption process, we failed to pay full attention to the information we received.

Luckily, we are both fairly open-minded people. (Besides, neither one of us wanted to make a scene by getting up to leave.) Most important, Jim's explanations really made sense. He answered all the arguments we had heard against open adoption. At that point we had had no close contact with either birthparents or adoptive families. We hadn't really thought about what the birthparents must go through. Why should they believe it when an agency worker tells them their baby is going to a "good home"? How much easier it would be to actually see that good home for themselves. And the ability to *choose* that home and family would give them at least a little control over an otherwise helpless situation.

The argument that if they knew where the baby was they would be likely to come and "steal him away" no longer made sense. Today, a persistent and resourceful birthparent could find out that information even with traditional adoption. With open adoption, we wouldn't have to worry about any surprise visits. And letting the birthparents participate in deciding where their baby would grow up should make it much less likely that they would want to remove a child from that chosen environment. The fact that we might be able to see and care for that baby at birth or soon after was appealing, in contrast to the normal three- to four-month wait with the traditional method. Within two hours that "crazy open adoption outfit" became, to us, the only sensible way to go.

Now all we had to do was complete the forms and interviews, and wait to see whether or not we would be accepted by the agency. Our hope that birthparents would welcome a doctor and a nurse for potential parents was quickly shot down by Jim. He told us that if we were approved, we should prepare ourselves for a longer than average wait. Doctors, he said, are often perceived as intimidating and as less than perfect parents because of their long work hours and time away from home. When we were approved, we kept that in mind but it didn't make the wait any easier.

Despite the fact that we knew adoption generally took three to five years and that we were told this particular process might take one and one-half years, the days became endless. We had just begun this at the end of July but in October Jim told our group that there were suddenly several possible babies soon to be born. What a day! We ran out and bought furniture, wallpaper, and essential supplies. One couple in our group became parents of a beautiful baby girl. We were ready to be next. We stayed near the phone or left forwarding phone numbers with the agency. And we waited. Jim told us that he had never told a group to get prepared like that before, and later said he would never do it again. For various reasons, the rest of those babies were not placed with couples in our group.

So we prepared again for a longer wait. But, early in the new year (1985), *the* call came. Jim said a young girl from out of town was expecting in mid-January and had chosen us as potential parents for her baby. Jim went on to describe "Lindsay" as a somewhat shy, soft-spoken, very bright and beautiful young woman. She was a member of the National Honor Society, had been on the honor roll in school, and was a cheerleader. She was 18 years old and had graduated from high school the previous June. Her plans for college were temporarily postponed due to this pregnancy, but she had taken some courses at the college in her hometown that fall. She had been dating her boyfriend "seriously" for over a year and a half and had known him for six years. "John" had also finished high school in June and was working in their hometown. Her family was very close and supportive.

As Jim went on to tell us more about them, the excitement was apparent in his voice. "You've really got a special one, here," he said. "I know you're really going to like Lindsay and her family." At that point, though, she did not want any direct contact with us, but Jim said he thought she might change her mind.

Were we excited? We were finally "expecting" and the due date was only about ten days away! Jim had said "she's fairly sure" that this is what she wants to do. We heard those words and knew we should prepare ourselves for the possibility that she might change her mind. That is one of the risks with open adoption, since our relationship with the birthparents often begins prior to the baby's birth. Once that baby is born, their resolve to release that now real and beautiful baby often falters. We knew all of this, but euphoria easily overtook any restraint on our part.

Lindsay did agree to talk to us by phone. Prior to that call several worries went through our minds—how did she really feel about this? Would she like us? Would we measure up to her expectations? Most of these thoughts were calmed with that first call. She was just like Jim had described. And her primary hope seemed to be that we might be able to give her baby some of the things she wanted for it but was currently unable to provide herself. Then she sent a picture of herself and John. She was beautiful and John looked surprisingly similar to pictures of Mike at that age. How lucky we were!

Now we could really get ready. We told our family and friends and the news quickly spread throughout the hospital. And we waited. As is common with the first baby, that due date came and went. Then, a full two weeks later, the phone rang in the middle of the night. This is not an uncommon occurrence at our house but Mike's normally groggy response was different this time. In an awe-filled voice he quietly said, "We have a baby girl!" and then louder, "A baby *girl!*"

Well, that was the end of any restful sleep for that night . . . and for a few months to come, for that matter. Of course, he had forgotten to ask anything else and we could hardly wait to call back at a more reasonable hour to find out all of the details. Lindsay had a healthy, 9-pound baby and both she and the baby were doing well. We held our breath for the next three days waiting to go down and see them. Those were three long days for us but it was Lindsay and her family's short time to spend with that baby.

On Saturday morning, we got up early and drove down there with Jim. I wished we could get there faster, yet I dreaded that moment of Lindsay's impending loss. By this time we had also gotten to know her mother a little and this would be her first grandchild. Everyone had been wonderful to us and had gone out of their way to make us feel welcome and comfortable but it was clear that this had been a very difficult situation for all of them.

As we approached her room, we saw a young man enter— that must be her 15-year-old brother, we thought. Then we learned that he was John. He looked so young! We quickly met Lindsay, her mother, and her sister. Lindsay was even prettier than in her picture. Her mom and sister were both vivacious and outgoing. The closeness in their family was readily apparent. Lindsay's love for that baby was also easy to see in her eyes. The baby was gorgeous! We couldn't take our eyes off of her either.

Everyone started talking at once. The baby needed a name. We had decided on "Lauren Elizabeth" and that seemed agreeable to them. We spent a few hours with all of them, getting to know each other a little better. Everyone took turns holding Lauren. The atmosphere was generally upbeat—there was a lot of humor and kidding around. John, especially, seemed to be the brunt of much of the ribbing but he appeared to be quite used to that. They were all wonderful in trying to make us feel comfortable and welcome. Lindsay was amazingly strong. Her mother and sister occasionally tearfully left the room for short periods but Lindsay held up until that last moment. As they got ready to leave, everyone hugged and kissed and said good-bye to us and Lauren. That good-bye was very hard but perhaps knowing they would see her again softened it just a little.

We had made plans to see them when Lindsay and her mother came up for the court hearing. The first date was cancelled due to a snowstorm but was rescheduled for the following week. The visit went very well. Lindsay was a bit hesitant and nervous about holding Lauren at first but did fine with just a little encouragement. She still seemed pretty restrained.

We exchanged letters fairly frequently at first and we sent piles of pictures. In the spring, Lindsay's mother came up with a friend who had business here and I took Lauren out to meet them. Then, in July, Lindsay and John both came for a visit. They were two hours late and it sounded like John was more than a little reluctant about the trip and visit. Other than that day, we have never heard from him. He was unusually quiet and quite hesitant around Lauren. Lindsay, on the other hand, seemed anxious and willing to hold and play with Lauren. Her earlier hesitation was almost completely gone. Later, Lindsay told us that this visit was a turning point in her feelings about the adoption. After that time, she was less depressed and better able to put that behind her and get on with her present life. She went away to college in the fall and, judging by the decreased frequency of her letters and the news we heard from her mother, she was enjoying the normal college activities.

We saw Lindsay and her family the first Christmas and again this year during the holidays. It was wonderful to see Lindsay's reaction to how much Lauren has changed in the past year. They played together and Lauren kept taking her around to see all of her toys and books. "Sit *here*, Lindsay!", she'd say, "Play my legos, read this book," etc., or just " Sit with me, Lindsay." They played and laughed together for several hours. Lauren doesn't know how Lindsay is related to her, of course, but she does know that she is someone who cares about her quite a lot. That alone is a big plus for open adoption.

In the past year, Lindsay has been very busy with school activities and travels. Still, she makes time to see Lauren when she can. We look forward to her next visit but we are glad she is able to do some of the things we both enjoyed so much when we were in college. Those were special times for us and we hope they will be special for her, too. She has made our present life more meaningful than words can ever express.

Robin and Lee Cottrell

"Love and trust for one another"

As I sit with my husband Lee and watch our daughter blowing out the two candles on her birthday cake, my mind is hit with memories like waves washing the shore line. Has it really been two years? I listen to the waves and watch the pictures pounding inside my head. Back, back I go and again it's October, 1983, and I'm waking up in the hospital and I know it's true. Six years and eight operations, with endless tests and so much pain, have put an end to hope. I now know I will never have a baby growing in my body, a body which I feel has failed me. I finally know it's time to look for another alternative.

Adoption, our only hope! Where do we go, whom do we talk to? First thing we consider is time. What's the fastest route to go? Foreign, hard-to-place children, or maybe private adoption? I'm so empty inside. Please, God, show me the way. Let me find a child that needs us as much as we need it. First we check out foreign adoptions, long-distance phone calls, sending for brochures, and meeting people who have gone this route. Next, we look into a local agency, we leave with our name on a long list—seven years, we are told. That's forever. I think, how can we bear it? Already I'm avoiding my pregnant girlfriends and their baby showers. I cry over diaper commercials and avoid our spare bedrooms. The search continues and I find another agency in the phone book that deals with adoption: Community, Family and Children Services.

Lee and I take a drive to Traverse City and stop in. We're in luck—within the month they're having an orientation meeting and we're invited to attend. On January 30, 1985, we are sitting in a meeting room with just two other couples and in walks the case-worker, Jim Gritter. He looks so young, I think, and ordinary, and he immediately puts us all at ease with his sense of humor. He starts explaining to us the concept of open adoption and right away warn-ing bells are going off in my head. How can this work? Having had six foster children in the past two years, we've known the pain of loving and nurturing these children, only to have them taken back and given to their natural parents. My mind just refused to hear anymore that evening and we left feeling very disappointed.

Two nights later, while watching our favorite television program: *20/20*, I sat up on the edge of the couch and grabbed Lee's hand. There was Jim Gritter and he was talking about this open adoption—not only he but the adoptive couple, their child, and the birthmother. They all seemed so relaxed and pleased with each other! We were hooked, and the next week we attended our first group meeting. This time there were eleven couples, two who had already adopted. We listened to their stories and were even more sure this program was the answer for us. Not only was it possible to have a child within two years but a newborn baby! A baby—oh, how I'd dreamed of nurturing and loving a real honest-to-goodness baby. Please, God, let these people find us to be an eligible adop-tive couple. We'll be the best mommy and daddy ever.

Within two seeks, we were told that we were eligible and could now go on to the next step—the home study. There was a moun-tain of paperwork. Questions and more questions. When will it stop? I began to get angry. Who were these people to judge whether or not we would make good parent material? We just knew they couldn't find better parents than Lee and I. Who made these peo-ple God, that they could wipe out our life's dream by the single word "no"? Life seemed so unfair at that time. Across the street was a family far larger than they could afford. Why are you being so unfair? I would ask God. Daily, the papers told of abused and murdered children, and here we sat with a nice home, lacking even one child. Why? Finally, around April, we completed the last of all those hated questions and were told that we were approved. So it was time to be patient and wait to be selected.

In May, the first couple in our group got a beautiful baby boy. Of course, I was happy for the lucky couple, but I knew in my heart that no one could possibly want or need a child as desperately as we did. We looked for ways to help pass the long wait . . . A weekend trip downstate and we had a beautiful furnished nursery. The chest of drawers began to fill with blankets, crib sheets, and little undershirts. I would spend hours washing little nightgowns and remaking the crib and baby cradle and I would cry. How much longer could I wait and still remain sane? We read books on baby care; yes, we would be perfect parents.

While I was trying to get pregnant, I had decided that I would breast-feed all of my children and I still hadn't let go of that dream. I would think, maybe I don't have a womb, but I still have breasts and God gave me those for a purpose. I called the nearest La Leche League and asked if they could send me some reading material on nursing the adopted child. Also, Jim Gritter gave me the name of a woman who had nursed not one, but two, of her adopted babies! Yes, it can be done, I was told, but you must be determined and have a lot of patience. Lee was very supportive of the idea and encouraged me to give it a try. I sent for a Lact-Aid kit which enables a baby to receive formula through a tube at the same time he nurses. I was enormously pleased to know that I would be contributing so vitally to the nourishing of my child. So there we were—a furnished nursery, breasts ready to receive a baby—but no baby.

By this time, two other couples had gotten their miracle phone call. What's wrong with us? Is it the town where we live? Is our house not grand enough? Doesn't Lee make enough money? All these doubts turned in my head like a merry-go-round.

On July 31st the phone rings! "Hello, Robin, this Jim Gritter." Oh, my God, is this it? I think. "I have a question to ask. We have a birthmother ready to deliver soon and you and Lee are one of the couples she is considering. We need to know if you and Lee would be prejudiced toward a baby of mixed blood. The birthfather is Persian."

"Of course not," I tell Jim, "I was once engaged to a guy from Iran myself."

"Okay," he said, "that's all I need to know. We'll know her decision by Thursday."

I asked Jim if he would please call even if the answer was no. He agreed and we hung up. Those three days passed like three long years. Everybody kept telling us not to get our hopes up, but somehow, inside, I had this feeling that our time had finally come.

Down to the store I went and purchased some more baby night-gowns, diapers, and nursing blouses. And we waited and calmed each other with our love. Thursday morning, not being able to stand the tension by myself (Lee, of course, had to go to work), I asked Linda, a girlfriend, to come sit with me to help pass the time. I was a basket case, so excited and yet scared the answer would be no. Please, Jim, hurry and call, I would say to the still phone. I paced the floor, drank endless cups of coffee, and found my eyes filling more than once. Linda did her best to calm me but she herself was nearly as excited. The time was passing and, having a family herself, Linda decided she'd better go do some errands. So, with a hug for luck, she and her daughter left.

As they were pulling out of the drive, the phone rang! I frantically waved her to come back and ran to the phone. I waited with my fingers crossed for the second ring—mustn't let them think I was sitting by the phone!

"Hello?" How can I sound so calm when my insides felt like jelly?

"Hello, is this Robin Cottrell?" asked a young-sounding girl.

"Yes, this is Robin," I answered.

"My name is Nancy, and Jim Gritter said I should be the one to call." I could tell by her hesitant voice that she was as nervous as I was. "I would like to ask if you and Lee would be the parents to my baby?"

"Yes, yes oh yes!" I'm crying and laughing. "You have just made us the happiest couple on earth," I tell her.

The tears are falling and my girlfriend is hanging on my neck, jumping up and down. I don't remember exactly what else was said, but then we were both so shy and so very nervous. Nancy told me that she was on her way to the hospital within the next couple of hours and would be delivering her baby by C-section at 8:00 A.M. the next morning. She would call and let us know what we had the minute it was possible. I thanked her the best way I knew how and hung up. Oh, my God, I'm going to be somebody's mommy; not next year or even next week, but tomorrow. I felt like Easter, Christmas, my birthday, and 4th of July was happening all at once!

My first call was to the radio operator where Lee works. I asked him to please raise Lee on his truck radio and tell him it's thumbs up! Next, I called my mother. When she came on the line, I said, "Hi, grandma!"

She squealed and said, "Really, you mean it?"

"Yes, it's true," I said, and started to cry again.

"When?" she asks.

"Tomorrow, Mom, tomorrow I'm gonna be a mommy!"

She was laughing and crying and kept repeating, "Really, tomorrow, really?"

The rest of the afternoon was spent making more phone calls and waiting for Lee to come home. I remember his truck pulling up in the driveway and my flying out the door into his outstretched arms, tears pouring down our cheeks and mingling together. I stepped back and looked into his eyes and said, "Welcome home, Daddy!"

That night, being too excited to stay home, we decided to go out and celebrate our pregnancy with all of our friends. We went to a local bar and about twenty of our friends were there to greet us. There were lots of kisses and hugs, back-slapping and teasing, drinks bought for us; the band dedicated songs and, of course, bets were made on the sex of the baby. It was a wonderful celebration and helped pass the long night.

We slept very little that night, and we were awake long before 8:00 A.M. We stayed in bed with the phone within arm's reach awaiting the call! We laughed, we cried a little, we hugged a lot, had coffee in bed, and still the phone didn't ring. All kinds of thoughts ran through our minds. What if something went wrong in delivery? What if, after Nancy saw the baby, she decided to keep it and was afraid to call and tell us? What if, what if? At 10:30 A.M., the phone rang. It was Nancy. We had ourselves a healthy 7 lb. 10 oz. baby girl!

We'd decided long before that, if it was a girl, we would call her Autumn Leigh. Nancy had chosen another name equally as pretty but decided Autumn would be put on the birth certificate. Nancy was exhausted and we didn't keep her on the phone long. We set Sunday, August 5th, as our meeting date because Nancy lived out of state and it would be several hours of driving for us.

More phone calls to our parents, sisters, my brother, aunts, uncles, cousins, our grandmothers, and all our friends. How wonderful, a little girl! She would be the first granddaughter on both sides of the family. A true miracle, a gift right from Heaven.

We went to Traverse City that afternoon to meet with Jim and get the background information on Nancy and he warned us again how Nancy could still change her mind and decide to keep Autumn. On the way home, we stopped by my mother's office and were congratulated by all the office help. My sister ran out from the shop out back and nearly knocked me down she was so excited.

I looked at my mom sitting behind her desk and burst into tears. "Oh Mom," I wailed, "I want to hold my baby so bad!" She came out from behind the desk and took me in her arms and let me sob. Before I knew it, I had the whole office in tears. We decided to depart on Saturday and spend the night with some friends who lived within an hour's driving distance from the hospital. My family gave us a little farewell party and gifts for the baby.

On Sunday, August 5th, at 1:00 P.M., we pulled into the hospital parking lot with our hearts pounding between our ribs and our hands clinging to one another. The desk clerk greeted us cheerfully and gave us the directions to Nancy's floor. On the elevator, we eyed each other critically and decided that our appearances were fine. Down the long corridor we walked on rubber legs at a fast pace. Outside Nancy's door we stopped, drew a deep breath and knocked. We heard a sweet voice ask us to come in. We paused, hugged tightly for a second, and entered the room. Sitting up in bed was a young, attractive woman with enormous blue eyes and a warm smile. Out of the corner of my eye I could see the baby's bed, but caution told me to go easy and I walked over to Nancy first and kissed her. Lee gave his hugs and, together, we approached the baby's bed. I turned to Nancy and asked her permission to hold the baby, as Jim had warned us about a birthmother's protective instincts. As I lifted her, I cooed and said what a beautiful baby she was and then turned to Nancy with tearfilled eyes and said, "I don't feel empty any more."

She smiled and said, "I'm so happy for you both."

I reluctantly handed Autumn to Lee and let him know the warmth of this little miracle. After Lee put her back in my arms, I asked Nancy if I could unwrap her blankets, and then began to study her perfect little body. I counted her fingers and toes, felt her heart beating and rained kisses on her tiny face. All the while, Nancy sat in her bed and beamed at us. We spent a good two hours getting to know each other.

When Autumn woke up and demanded to be fed, I asked if I could nurse her as I'd brought the Lact-Aid with me. Nancy was quite excited and encouraged me to do so. She buzzed for a nurse and explained what I wanted to do. I fear that the nurse was a little shocked and went out to consult with another nurse. This was the hospital's first experience with open adoption so they thought we were all a little crazy to begin with. Soon they returned with a fresh bottle of formula and after I showed them how it would work, they left us to our privacy. I took Autumn in my arms, guided her mouth to my nipple, and inserted the tube. Autumn began sucking greedily and Nancy and I shared a look I'll never forget. I feel this is the exact moment our love and trust began for one another. Her eyes told me, yes, I know you will love my baby and my eyes telling her, thank you for this little Heaven's Treasure. As I looked down at Autumn, she chose to open her eyes for the first time and love just filled my whole being so that, even now, I find that words are inadequate to describe it.

Shortly after Autumn was fed and changed, there was a knock at the door and Nancy's mother walked in. She was, by far, the most nervous of us all, but soon relaxed and we enjoyed another hour or so visiting. Much too soon the nurse came in and said it was time for Autumn to be returned to the nursery. Oh, how I hated that. We decided it would be best, however, if we left. We'd been there for over four hours! We said our goodbyes with promises to return the next day. Of course, on our way out, we stopped by the nursery and watched Autumn through the window.

On Monday, we returned to the hospital and I was disappointed to learn that we'd just missed Autumn's feeding. I was already feeling quite possessive, but was content just holding her. We only stayed a short while because Nancy was feeling sore and tired. She asked us to please not come the next day because she needed at least one day alone with her baby. I tried not to show my disappointment. But we understood, and I felt such sorrow and compassion for this brave young woman.

On Tuesday, all my old fears came back to torment me and even Lee was unable to comfort me. I was feeling so selfish and forgot for a moment the mental anguish Nancy must be going through. I sat next to the phone and refused to move until after Nancy called. Our friends suggested taking a ride or going shopping. It had begun to rain. I just wanted to be left alone.

Jim called us to see how we were doing and I told him about my fears. He said that he'd just gotten through talking to Nancy and, although he couldn't say for sure, he thought she was still going to go through with it. He also told us to be prepared in case she decided to keep the baby. We'd always known this was one of the risks of open adoption. If that happened, we decided, we'd treat it as we had our miscarriage.

Finally, at 6:30, Nancy called, sounding very cheerful. She said that the hospital was releasing her and the baby tomorrow and we could pick Autumn up at her sister Sue's home. We'd been having extremely dry, hot weather the last few days and now relief poured through me like the rain that was now flooding the grass outside. After I hung up the phone, Lee, our friends, and I went out on the porch and let the rain drench us. My black mood left me like the storm clouds passing overhead.

Wednesday morning Lee and I were both in a frenzy. We packed and unpacked the baby's bag several times, fussed over our appearance, snapped at one another, and finally we left the safety of our friend's home and were on our way to Sue's house. Nancy's mother greeted us warmly in the driveway and led us into the house. There we were properly introduced to Sue. Nancy came forward from the living room and I saw that her big blue eyes were red and swollen from crying. She managed to give us a trembling smile and my heart fell into a million pieces. With our arms around one another, we walked over to Autumn's bassinet and stood looking down at her. I can only imagine what was happening inside Nancy's head. I wanted to scream . . . . I hurt so bad for this woman.

We were invited to sit down and have a glass of iced tea with them. After we'd been talking for a while, Sue left the room and returned with a pile of gifts and set them down in front of us. These people never ceased to amaze us with the love and generosity they were showering on us when I felt it should be the other way around. It was getting late in the afternoon and, as Lee and I had a long drive ahead of us, I knew the time had come to take the big step. Time to say our goodbyes . . .

Nancy walked over and picked up Autumn as her sister and mother discreetly left the room. Nancy turned to us with Autumn in her arms, kissed her and, as she put her in my arms, broke down and started sobbing. Now, this was more than I could handle and I tried to give her back the baby. I said, "I can't do this to you; please don't make me be the cause of all this pain. No papers have been signed; she's still yours!" Nancy just shook her head and said that she knew she was doing the best thing for Autumn and all she asked was that we take good care of her and love her.

How do you convince a mother that you will love and cherish her child like no other child has been loved before? Words are inadequate at a time like this, so I just hugged her tight and whispered "I will" and left quickly. Lee held on to Nancy and I could hear them both sobbing as I left. I walked down the steps to find Sue and her mother crying quietly in the back yard. I went to Nancy's mother and she held me as I cried for her daughter. Soon Lee and Nancy stepped outside and, with tears streaming down all our faces, Lee and I took that precious baby and left.

But that day wasn't the end of the story; it was only the beginning. Because Nancy lives out of state, I regret to say that she has only been able to visit four times in the past two years. She comes for week-long stays and it's always hard to let her go. Not only do we have a beautiful daughter, but Nancy is a part of our family now, too. We spend those visits getting to know each other better and we laugh and cry together. We talk about our dreams and fears for Autumn and about Nancy's future plans. She recently graduated from college and I was able to attend her graduation and meet some more of her family members. Between visits, we write long letters and tape videos of Autumn for her. I keep her up to date on all of Autumn's new accomplishments and also share accounts of her occasional orneriness and bull-headedness. I send bundles of pictures and phone her often. We don't want her to miss out on anything.

Autumn knows Nancy as a special friend and is always excited to see her come. I tell her she grew in Nancy's belly and that she's adopted, but of course she's too young to understand all this. She knows she is a loved child and is a very happy and loving little girl in return. I believe Autumn has a heart big enough to love all members of her birthfamily as well as her adoptive family. It's been hard for all of Autumn's grandparents to accept this open adoption, but I believe, in time, they'll see that this is right for Autumn and that her life is enriched because of it.

So now, as I watch Autumn blow out her birthday candles and look up at me with those blue eyes like bits of the sky, I silently thank Nancy for her gift of love, and I know the true meaning of fulfillment.

Lynne and Rick Nolan

"A generous gift from Jill"

We had been married three years and after many tests we were told that our best chance to have children was to adopt. Rick and I both wanted children very much, so we checked with a number of agencies and considered different forms of adoption. Finally, in the fall of 1982, we narrowed it to the two local agencies and were put on their lists of people waiting for the next orientation meeting.

In January, notices came from both agencies and we excitedly attended both meetings. It was interesting to note their differing philosophies: one practiced open adoption and the other a closed approach. We talked it over and opted to go with the open agency as it struck us as a kind and caring way to go about the experience.

We attended three educational meetings with other prospective adoptive parents. We met some very nice people and became friends with them. After the three meetings, we were asked once again if we wanted to continue. We did. Now came the family studies which involved a lot of worksheets, conferences with Jim, our social worker, preparation of a family tree, and decisions about how much openness to offer. We were really kept busy.

Finally came the wonderful news that we were approved by the agency. We still had some more meetings to go to, but we felt some relief. The meetings with our peers were fun and we drew close to each other. While attending the meetings we felt that we were actively advancing our cause, but next came the passive phase of waiting for something to happen. Waiting is probably the most difficult part of the experience. We had less contact with the agency, and so it was hard to know how "ready" we should be. It had been eight months since we attended our first meeting and time seemed to be going fairly quickly.

About two weeks after being approved, Jim called to see if we would be interested in a 6-month-old boy. "A real charmer" were his words. A meeting was scheduled for the next day with his birthmother. Wow! So soon? We were speechless. We were shaking our heads in disbelief.

We were at the agency a little early; she was a little late. She had packed all of Tommy's clothes and some of his toys so the transition would go smoothly. She was quiet for the most part and it was obvious she loved this beautiful little boy. We thought we were prepared for this, but it was far more powerful than we expected. She was sad and we were sad with her. There were many tears shed that day.

There was a gamble built into our agreement to take Tommy. With openness, there is an effort to minimize the amount of disruption the baby experiences. In this state, most children who are adopted are first routed into a foster home. In our instance, you might say we were our own foster home. When we accepted Tommy into our home and hearts, we knew it was still possible for his birthmom to change her mind.

All the baby paraphernalia that Tommy's birthmom sent with him was a great help. What didn't come with him, our family was quick to supply. Tommy had a hard time at first. He didn't sleep well at night and he didn't look happy. He missed his mom. We were sad that he was sad but we realized things would get better with time. In the meantime, we just loved him for all we were worth and hoped he would accept our love. After a week went by, things had pretty well settled down. We knew that it was getting close to the time for his birthmom to go to court and figured we would hear from the agency any day. Finally we did, but the news wasn't what we wanted to hear. She simply couldn't go through with it and all the while she had been apart from Tommy, she had been heartbroken and miserable. Jim would be by to pick up Tommy the next day.

Even though we should have known better, we were shocked. The truth is, our first reactions were bitter. How could she do this to us? What happened to her reasons? Didn't she like us?

That night we packed up all his things. I felt bad for Rick and he felt bad for me. We said our goodbyes to this sweet little boy who, with his big brown eyes, had so quickly stolen our hearts. We couldn't help but wonder if his birthmother changed her mind because she had not designed a plan with enough openness in it. If only she had gotten to know us better and watched our interaction with Tommy. If only she had seen the way Rick and Tommy looked at each other. . . . Our only consolation was our knowledge that Tommy and his mom really loved each other.

The most difficult part of the experience was telling our family and friends what had happened. We must have explained it four thousand times and each time we felt bad because they would feel bad. They told us that things would work out because "God had something in mind for us."

After that experience, we decided to play it a little safer next time. We thought, "Let's have the papers signed by the birthparents *before* we take the baby into the family."

Our group was still getting together once in awhile and some of the couples were experiencing success. We took heart in their relatively less complicated experiences. It was getting close to Christmas and we figured for us it would be another childless holiday season.

How wonderful it is sometimes to be wrong! The call came on December 22nd and the invitation was to come and pick up a little boy at 4 o'clock the next day. Could we make it? Silly question. Ryan was 2½ months old and the papers had been signed. We first met him at his foster parents' home and, in the process, got to know his foster mother, Mrs. Popp. She is a wonderful, loving lady and we have stayed in touch with her over the years.

So we were parents at last. There is no way to begin to describe our elation. We were a little disappointed, though, that Ryan's birthmother, Andrea, had not chosen to meet us. That made us feel a little bit left out and we were more than a little envious of the friendships with birthparents that other adoptive parents were describing.

We decided to do something about it and wrote Andrea a letter expressing our wish to meet with her. Happily she accepted our invitation and we were able to spend some time with her. We remain in close contact with her and feel fortunate to have such a connection.

When Ryan turned two years old, we decided to put our name in again. The second time there was much less rigamarole and it seemed like we were back in the waiting pattern in almost no time at all.

Waiting was still a difficult time, but with Ryan at our side, it wasn't quite as hard on us as it had been previously. We decided once again that we would take the risk of welcoming a child into our home prior to the birthmother's signing the papers. It is a gamble which usually works out and, when it works, it is truly a wonderful way to go. On the other hand, we knew better than most how difficult it can be if the gamble backfires. We figured the risk was worth it and that our chances of getting burned twice were pretty small. But, of course, you never know.

1986 brought us lots of good news. The year was hardly underway and Rick was starting a good new job. Then Jim called to inform us that we could shortly expect an important call. Sure enough, five minutes later Jill called. I was a little worried that I wouldn't know what to say, but the words came easily. She noted that she was due in a few weeks and was eager to meet us. We made arrangements to meet the next day. Since she was scheduled for an ultrasound, we decided to meet her at the hospital.

"Everything is fine," she told us when we found each other that next day. She knew the sex of the baby, but we elected to live with the suspense of not knowing. We went to her sister's house, where she was staying during her pregnancy, and had an emotional heart-to-heart talk. We seemed to understand each other almost immediately, each of us showing concern for what this experience might mean for the other. She invited us to be part of the labor and delivery experience. This touched us deeply for we knew that this is truly an intimate moment. We also knew that it was a moment we would never experience unless it came as a generous gift from someone like Jill.

The hours passed quickly and soon her sister and family came home from work. They insisted we stay for supper. We shared some festive pizza and laughter in equal portions. Jill told us she was pleased she had chosen us and that she would stand firm in her resolve to go ahead with adoption. We wished the occasion could last forever, but it had gotten late and we left with many tears and many hugs. No matter what the ultimate outcome, this had been one of the most remarkable days of our lives. We drove home exhausted, feeling oddly elated and sad at the same time.

The call to action came about three weeks later. I was told not to rush since progress was slow. I thought to myself, "Lynne, how are you *not* going to rush in circumstances like these?" Since Rick's new job made it impossible for him to be there, I called my mother to join me for moral support. You never know when you might need a shoulder and I wanted one close at hand.

Arriving at the maternity floor, I was met by a person I took to be a nurse. But she introduced herself as Jill's mother and indicated she was there to help also. As I.changed into hospital garb, I issued a prayer for Jill and the baby and me.

To say the least, Jill was not enjoying labor. She was getting mighty tired of it and was no longer shy about saying so. When it came time for delivery, Jill's mother and I were nearly as pleased to see the doctor as was Jill. I knew he was supportive of the adoption plan. He turned to Jill's mother and asked, "How's this going to work?" She said, "I stay with Jill; Lynne goes with the baby."

The end was in sight and our excitement was growing. I stayed at Jill's side and in a matter of minutes, the baby was born. *It's a boy!* The tears wouldn't stop. I wanted to pinch myself. Surely all this could not be true. I watched as the nurse weighed, measured, and bathed him. While all this was happening, he was exercising his lungs. Finally, I got to hold him. He was so tiny and it suddenly occurred to me that I already loved him.

Jill's first plan was to not see him. It was her decision, of course, but I hoped she would decide to spend some time with him. About an hour after he was born, she did ask to see him. She was strong and kept her composure. She was steadfast in her plan and, the next day, this remarkable lady went home with empty arms.

When Rick arrived that first night, he was wound up. There are not very many men in this world with more love for children than Rick has. He was greeted, however, with some worrisome news. The baby's latest check-up had discovered an irregular heartbeat and an elevated blood count. The doctor felt tests were in order and that antibiotics should be started as a precautionary measure. We were worried for awhile but, thank God, they never found anything.

We called him Matthew and, on the third day, we took him home with us. It was good to be home so we could love him without interruption. We were pleased to see that Ryan seemed to approve of the new addition to the family.

We kept in contact with Jill to keep her informed and let her know we had not forgotten her. She said that she was doing fine and was looking forward to going to court to get everything behind her.

But when Jill's court date arrived, things were different. She had had a long talk with the birthfather and had changed her mind. She wanted Matthew back. She didn't call us; Jim did.

I took the news without comment, because I had no voice to comment with. I called Rick at work and he was completely devastated. He bolted for home. When the call had come asking for Tommy's return, it had hurt beyond description. We didn't think it could hurt any worse than that, but this time, we discovered new depths of pain and anguish. This was pain times ten.

We gathered some of Matthew's things and put them in a bag. We wrote a page describing his routine so that the transition would go as smoothly as possible.

When we arrived at the agency a couple of hours later, we hoped we would be able to see Jill and talk with her, but she wasn't there. Jim was to bring Matthew to her. Tearfully we said our goodbyes, not really understanding why she had changed her mind and why this was happening to us again. At times like this, Jim's job is extremely difficult. His face was covered with tears, he felt so bad for us.

It was a very long ride home and we knew some difficult times awaited us. We were already exhausted and now we had the countless explanations to make once again, not to mention putting away the baby paraphernalia.

Later that evening, we decided to call Jill to see how she was doing. She had left a letter for us which helped a little, but we were still worried about Matthew and her. It took a lot of nerve to call but, finally, we did. . . . No answer. We decided to let it be at that, it was none of our business anyway. At that time, we realized more than ever before how important it is to be able to communicate with the other people involved.

We cried ourselves to sleep and slept deeply, but the next morning with all its explanations was simply terrible. We hugged Ryan tightly. Without really knowing what was going on, he said, "Don't cry, Mommy and Daddy; it will be alright."

In that day's mail, we received the hospital pictures. They were so cute, but they did not belong to us. It was the perfect opportunity to call Jill and talk with her. Nervously, I dialed and this time there was an answer.

She didn't seem very happy.

"Matthew is okay, but he misses you."

"That's only normal since he was with us a couple of weeks. He'll get used to you quickly. It will just take a little time. It'll work out. The pictures from the hospital came today. Do you want me to send them to you or to the agency?"

"Keep them, Lynne. Keep them. I've made a big mistake. He belongs to you. I want you to come and pick him up." Jill was weeping and her tone of voice indicated she meant what she was saying.

Jill pushed aside all my protests and reassurances. She wanted to proceed with adoption. I was dumbfounded. I wasn't sure it was even possible any more and suggested she call Jim about it.

Once again, I was in a state of mind where I couldn't believe what was happening. Could it really be that we could get him back?

A long hour passed and the phone rang. It was Jim and he was wondering whether we were interested in taking Matthew again. Believe it or not, even though we loved Matthew with all our hearts, this was a difficult decision. Word got out about what was happening and everyone we knew was praying for us.

We decided yes. Yes, we would take our chances. Our hearts completely overruled the caution of our minds. We proceeded on faith and, within hours, had Matthew in our arms again. And, for those who may wonder about the power of prayer, we discovered that Jill had taken advantage of a cancellation at court to go in and sign the papers! The suspense was over and Matthew was ours to love.

Jill had left us a note and asked us to call. We did and we shared our feelings about this remarkable experience. We assured her that she was a welcome person in our lives, but she indicated a preference to keep the relationship one of letters and phone calls for the time being. We certainly wanted more but were willing to respect her wishes.

A couple of years have gone by now and we have a very happy family. To say the least, our adoption experiences have been very exciting and touching. We love to tell them to other people, most especially to other adoptive parents. We have not regretted any of our decisions. Would we do it again? You bet! As a matter of fact, we intend to!

We are committed to being honest with our birthparents. We strive to keep a good healthy relationship going with them. They will fill an important role in the lives of our children and we care for them deeply. We pray that God may richly bless them even as they and God have blessed us.

Cathy and Doug Lundy

"No one can possess another"

We left the meeting knowing we had to talk. The two-hour presentation at Community, Family and Children Services on open adoption was very different from what we had heard at other agencies, and we were startled. It seemed odd to us that something so unconventional could also be so sensible. We were intrigued, but skeptical. One thing we knew for sure: This provocative approach to adoption was worth a closer look.

As we attended more informational meetings, open adoption became a common phrase around our household. The more we learned about it, the better it looked. The birthparents would have no questions as to the whereabouts or condition, growth, and development of the child. The child would know of the adoption and would not have questions about his background in later years, and we, as the adoptee's parents, would not have to hide the fact of the child's adoption, and could establish a friendship with the birthparents that the child could continue in later years. All of this sounded so good to us that we sometimes wondered if we were imagining it. We decided to be as open as the birthparents wished and step back should they, or we, feel the need to do so.

We discovered the rumor that there is lots of paperwork built into the adoption process was not only true, it was understated. Actually we didn't mind because the questions usually covered pertinent territory and we enjoyed clarifying and sharing our thoughts on the issues. We worked hard on the portfolio of information the agency uses to acquaint birthparents with potential adoptive parents because this was an opportunity to advance our cause. In most forms of adoption, adoptive parents are completely dependent and helpless, but with openness we were responsible for our own "chooseability." That gave us some sense of control over the situation.

As it turns out we were indeed chooseable; Brenda selected us not too long after we turned in our material. We arranged to meet her at her parents' home where she was staying the last weeks of her pregnancy. She was three weeks from her due date.

We arrived at the house with mixed emotions, eager and yet apprehensive at this first meeting. What if she didn't like us? Would she change her mind and choose someone else? What if we didn't like *her*? We knew that we had a say in this arrangement too. If we didn't feel compatible with her, we could call off the plan, but we knew that would be awkward. Our fears were soon allayed. As we sat and talked at the dining table, we were all put at ease by the conversation. We talked about everything: families, music, food, religion, education. At one point Brenda's mother paused and observed, "This meeting is amazing!" That summed up our feeling very well; to be meeting the birthmother of our future child (as well as her family who wandered by to inspect us) was not something one normally did when adopting a child. We left the meeting encouraged that all was going as planned. We felt her approval of us and we were certainly impressed with her. Soon we would become parents!

The next three weeks did not go by quickly. We knew Brenda could change her mind at any time, and spoke with her on that. She seemed steadfast in her decision to release the child, but we knew that once the child was a living person outside of her body, the decision would have to be made again.

Brenda went into labor on Monday, and Matthew arrived on Wednesday. We received a phone call from her mom, telling us all was well after a long labor. We waited until Friday to drive downstate. Although we were anxious to see and hold him, we wanted her to have time to do the same. The hardest part was yet to come.

The hospital was aware that we were coming and we met with their social worker, to whom all of this was new. We had been given a letter of introduction from the agency and after checking our identification, we were ushered up to the maternity ward. Matthew was sleeping in the nursery amongst all the other babies; it was hard to see him so close and not be able to touch him.

We soon found Brenda. She was in good spirits and more at ease than either of us would have been in her situation. It was important for her to see us interact with Matthew at the hospital. Although neither of us had much experience at handling a newborn, we were soon feeding and burping him, trying to keep him awake so we could see those beautiful blue eyes. The following two days, we returned to the hospital during visiting hours. The staff soon grew accustomed to us, but we could sense their skepticism as we walked down the hall.

During one of our visits, the birthfather, who lived out of state, called to speak with Brenda. He had originally directed Brenda to Community, Family and Children Services, knowing that adoption was the best alternative for all involved. Our conversation with him was somewhat strained, but we were pleased to have the contact. Our only other communication with him since then has been at Matthew's first birthday when we received a lovely card and letter. Should he wish to write, speak, or meet with us in the future, we are more than ready to do so.

Brenda wanted the baby to be named prior to his release from the hospital in order that the name be the same on both birth certificates. Initially, she wanted no part in choosing a name but when questioned again, responded by suggesting a middle name: James.

Matthew James and Brenda were to be released on the same day, Monday. On Sunday night we could hardly sleep and could only imagine Brenda's state of mind. She had given us a photo of Matthew, and we must have stared at it for hours. In order not to be disappointed, I was convinced that she would not release him.

Monday morning finally arrived. We greeted Brenda in her room, where she was gathering her belongings. Matthew was finally brought in and a nurse dressed him in a sleeper which we had provided for the trip home. The hour of reckoning had come and we were full of dread and anticipation. Could she hand over her baby to us after carrying him for nine months and giving birth to him? In order to ease her pain, Brenda said she visualized this scene many times over, but visualizing and actually participating in it were two different matters.

Brenda was escorted down the hall in a wheelchair, carrying Matthew, while we walked alongside with her mother. At the exit, the nurse assisted Brenda out of the wheelchair and began to hand the baby back to her. She responded by saying, "No, give the baby to Cathy and Doug." At this point, we couldn't comprehend how Brenda could be so strong as to watch two people drive away with her baby. We knew she could still change her mind until she went to court to finalize the adoption, but leaving the hospital seemed too final. All of us were in tears except Matthew, who was sleeping soundly, oblivious of this profound moment in his life.

We were elated to have Matthew home, but felt guilty at the same time. How could we accept this child whom we knew Brenda loved so much? We finally realized that we weren't the only ones who loved Matthew. He was not "our child"; no one can possess another. We would be there to guide him throughout his years, just as Brenda would have been had she not released him for adoption. There was room enough for all to love him.

The first several months following Matthew's birth, we were in contact quite often with Brenda. She came to our house after her "day in court" to sign final release forms for the baby. Although she had given up all legal claim to him that afternoon, there she was, holding him that evening.

Since then, we have corresponded, exchanging birthday greetings, Christmas cards, and day-to-day news. Phone calls usually precede a visit, which happens several times a year. Matthew is unaware at this point who Brenda really is; as he grows older we hope that he'll understand, and appreciate his extended family. We also have contact with Matthew's birthgrandparents. They enjoy photos of him as any grandparent would, and are appreciative of the contacts they have with him.

We are pleased that there is no mystery built into the fabric of Matthew's life. No matter what questions he may develop over time, we will be able to supply answers. Matthew's circumstances are no accident; his life has meaning. His birthmother loves him, and because of that love she carefully designed a plan to benefit him. We and Brenda appreciate each other and Matthew thrives as a result.

In early 1986 we decided to submit our names to Community, Family and Children Services to adopt a second child. Matthew would be two years old that fall, and we thought that was a good age span between siblings. There was no guarantee when we would be chosen, but we hoped it would be within the next year.

Our first group meeting was held at the agency in May of 1986 with approximately ten other couples present. This was a unique group of people for we had all previously adopted a child through the agency. In future meetings, we shared all that had been positive and negative in our first experiences with adoption. Even those who had suffered the sadness of a birthparent's change of heart were ready to try again. The positive aspects of open adoption far outweighed any negative feelings anyone had for the program.

We held our meetings informally at one another's homes every six to eight weeks. There was paperwork to update and a summary package to assemble again, including recent photos, three-page statement, openness checklist, home study, and a creative project. Our hopes were that the second adoption would be similar in openness to the first. In the future, we wanted both of our children to have a relationship with their birthmoms—it would be hard for one child to understand should his birthmom show no interest in him while the other was showered with cards, presents, and attention.

In mid-December, we received the long-awaited phone call from the agency: we had been chosen by Debbie, a single woman from the Detroit area. She was due January 10th, so Jim Gritter advised us to contact her soon regarding an initial meeting. He was also sending us forms Debbie had filled out, giving us some background information on her as well as on the birthfather.

We called Debbie and set up a meeting two days after Christmas at her mom's house. In reading over her application form, we immediately felt a rapport with her; her answers were intelligent, honest, and showed concern for her future child. She wanted a high degree of openness, as we did, with the option to step back should things not work out between us as anticipated.

We arrived as planned on Saturday morning. Our son, Matthew, age 2 ¼ years, came with us. Hopefully, he would put his best foot forward and lessen the tension for all. A child's remarks are so open and honest that one can't help but feel at ease. Debbie's mother, Judy, certainly made us feel very comfortable in her home. Conversation was not lacking, especially with a Christmas tree and a two-year-old around. We spoke of the upcoming birth and details pertaining to the hospital: when we'd be called, visiting the hospital, the child's release. Debbie was gracious enough to let Matthew feel her stomach, and we explained that the baby was in there and soon would come out. He remarked, "Make it come out!" which brought laughter from all of us. Since then, he has said he came out of Brenda's (his birthmom's) tummy and Nicole came out of Debbie's. Their birth story is often a part of his nightly bedtime routine.

We departed from Detroit hopeful that all would go as planned in the next several weeks, We kept in contact with Debbie. When her due date passed, we were just as anxious as she. We continued to talk to our son about the baby in Debbie's tummy that would soon come out. He was much relieved when we showed him the bassinet she would sleep in. In one storybook, brother bear had to give up his bed for his baby sister, and Matthew wanted no part of that.

At 10:30 P.M. on Thursday, January 22, 1987, Judy called to say that Debbie had given birth to a healthy baby girl that afternoon. We were both delighted at the thought of a daughter; Doug has two brothers and I have five, so a girl was definitely our first choice. We decided to name her after we saw her. We had several possibilities in mind, but we wanted to see what name "fit" her.

We talked with Debbie the next day; she seemed in good spirits and suggested we come to the hospital on Saturday. That gave her some time to reassess the situation and make her decision now that the baby was born.

We had made arrangements to stay with our son's birthgrandparents while in the Detroit area. So on Friday afternoon, we headed downstate. We were still in the midst of a winter blizzard and decided to start out while there was a lull in the storm. On Saturday, we arrived at the home of Teenie and Mike Romanchik. They were delighted to see Matthew and he, likewise, to see their selection of toys. They settled down to watch him while we visited the hospital that afternoon.

We arrived at the hospital and inquired at the main desk for the maternity floor. The receptionist asked what relation we were to Debbie. When Doug responded with "We hope to adopt the child," she seemed all flustered but responded with "Go right up." The hospital was aware that we were coming, but still it's quite a shock to some about how candid we are.

We stepped off the elevator on the maternity floor and ran right into Debbie, who was pushing the bassinet down the hall. She was very comfortable in our presence—much more so than when we first met. The baby was sleeping as only a newborn can. We spent several hours in Debbie's private room conversing, and officially named the baby Nicole Rose. She was beautiful! Judy arrived accompanied by her fiancé, George, and her sister to join in this celebration of new life.

Since Debbie had had no problems with the delivery, and Nicole was healthy, her doctor suggested the release could be the following day, Sunday. Originally, Debbie hoped that we could leave the hospital first with Nicole, then she would be discharged. But in order to do that, the hospital social worker would have to be present, and she was not available until Monday. So plan B was suggested: Debbie and Nicole would be discharged together and we would all meet at her mother's house.

We informed Jim Gritter of this arrangement. He originally planned to come down to ease the hospital release, but could not arrive until late afternoon on Sunday, so we suggested he stay home and take a much-deserved day off!

Sunday arrived. We had a lovely morning with our hosts, the

Romanchiks, and then departed to take the car seat and infant clothing to the hospital. Doug and Matthew visited in the lobby, our son exploring the surroundings as any two-year-old would. (To this day, when we tell Nicole's birth story, he talks about seeing his favorite muppets Ernie and Bert in the gift shop.) I delivered the clothing to Debbie's room and then departed while she dressed Nicole for her trip into the world.

We drove to Judy's house, where Leah, her other daughter, and a friend of Debbie's were waiting. Soon Debbie, Judy, and George arrived with Nicole. All were excited. Matthew exclaimed, "She's so teeny tiny! I want to touch her," which he did. So did everyone else. Nicole went from one loving arm to the next. Her great-grandmother arrived, as well as another close friend of Debbie's. Our quick stop stretched into several hours, but we felt very comfortable among our new extended family.

We eventually had to break away, and yet felt guilty about doing so. It was much more comfortable leaving from a private home than from the hospital door as we had done with our son, Matthew. Here, Debbie had much more support of family and friends and we, having experienced this situation once before, were now at ease and knew what to expect. But the emotions flowed freely on both sides.

We drove part way home that afternoon and spent the night at the home of Doug's parents, who were away in Florida. Family and friends were notified that we were now a family of four—or almost. Debbie still had to sign final release forms in court in several weeks.

Upon arriving home, we let Debbie know that all was well. That initial contact gave her some relief, to know that we did want to be open with her in the future. In several weeks, Debbie, Judy, Leah, and Shelly, Deb's aunt (who had also adopted through the agency), came to dinner at our home prior to the court date. We had a lovely evening, with Nicole the center of attention.

The following day, Debbie went before the judge in Traverse City. Although she was prepared for what would happen, the finality of the situation hit home. At least, should she desire, she could have contact with Nicole in the future. She had been a part of her life for nine months, and will continue to be so for the rest of her life.

We have had limited contact with Debbie during these first few months, mainly by letter with photos enclosed. We are but a phone call away should she desire to see Nicole, and just knowing that must ease her mind somewhat. Nicole has filled a void in our lives that only a baby can, and she is dearly loved by us as well as family and friends. She will know Doug and me as her parents, but will someday be aware of the role Debbie played in her creation, too.

Through our adoption experiences, we have been enriched in many ways. Our family has grown, not only with the addition of two children, but with the relationships that have developed with their birthmothers, birthgrandmothers, aunts and uncles. We feel very fortunate to have an agency such as Community, Family and Children Services in our area to assist those who wish to adopt openly. All those involved—the social workers, the birthparents, the parents — gain from the experience of seeing a child placed in a loving home with his roots clearly defined. Only time will tell how the children react to their situation, but if we are comfortable with it, we think their feelings will be similar. We are more than comfortable; we wouldn't have it any other way.

Mike and Jean Spry—II

"Worth the risk"

In this chapter, Mike writes about the second experience he and Jean had with openness in adoption. The names of many of the key people involved have been changed to protect their identities. The reader should also note that this situation was quite unusual and not typical of most releases in the program. What stands out, however, is Mike and Jean's solid commitment to the program throughout some very trying developments.

Our second encounter with openness in adoption started innocently enough. Ironically, I was talking to one of my former students about the part-time child-care leave I would be taking in anticipation of a possible adoption in the relatively near future. I was explaining to him how the dynamics of the program leave you guessing about when the adoption of your baby will actually occur. "It could be two years from now, next week, tomorrow—you never know."

Within two minutes our conversation was interrupted by the ringing of the telephone in my office; it was Abbie Nelson from the agency. She explained that there were two birthparents in her office who were anxious to speak with me. Heather came on the line and said that she and her boyfriend, Fred, wanted to meet Jean and me *very soon* because she was due to deliver her baby "anytime now." Talk about instant parenthood! The shock left me babbling for the rest of the day.

Thus began an emotional excursion like no other Jean and I had experienced. There is no way either of us could have known, going in, how mercurial this situation would become and the toll it would take on us as things developed. It certainly underscored the idea that each open adoption is very different.

Jean and I met the birthparents at our home on the evening following Abbie's phone call. It is a bit unusual to have the first meeting at the home of either party to the adoption, but through a series of circumstances, that is how it worked out in this case. Other than that, it was probably a fairly typical first meeting and went about as well as could be expected, It was clear from the onset that the birth would be very different from what we had experienced when Lara (our first child) was born. For starters, we would not be allowed to visit the baby in the hospital because of concerns over family tensions; while this was very understandable, it was nonetheless disappointing.

We found further disappointment in not being invited to participate in the naming of the baby. Even though we knew that we could later change the baby's name, we didn't really want to do that for fear it would be an affront to Heather or Fred. We just hoped that they would pick a name that we could live with. Also different this time around was the fact that both the birthfather and birthmother wanted to have an ongoing relationship with us after the birth.

One other interesting dynamic came to light during this first meeting. Fred made it quite clear that adoption was not his first choice of possible outcomes. He added, however, that Heather did not want to go along with his preferred plan, so he had accepted the fact that openness in adoption was the next best alternative. He felt that he would be able to release the baby when the time came, although he acknowledged that it would be difficult. He said that it would be very important for him to be able to trust the adoptive parents. We tried to ease his mind about our trustworthiness by offering the phone number of Lara's birthmother (Reneé) and suggesting that Heather or Fred call her. We also extended an open invitation for further contact before the birth so we could all get better acquainted.

On the afternoon following our initial face-to-face encounter, Jean and Heather got together again, and Jean was able to meet Heather's mother, a brother, and a sister. Throughout the discussions, Heather seemed very committed to the idea of releasing her baby. In general, circumstances appeared to be promising for us, although we readily and openly acknowledged that everything could change suddenly after the birth.

Our next significant contact did not occur until four days later when Abbie called to let us know that Heather had delivered a beautiful baby boy on the previous day. Abbie said that Heather was still intent on releasing the baby to us, but that Fred was "in orbit"—seemingly swept away by the magic and intensity of the moment. According to Abbie, Fred gave every appearance of trying to engineer the situation so that Heather would keep the baby. Abbie added that the baby (as yet unnamed) would be released from the hospital the next day and that we needed to be prepared to take him if everything suddenly fell into place. Noting the apparent strength of Heather's resolve to follow through with her plan, Jean and I figured that in all likelihood, Fred would once again be forced to confront the reality of the situation and acquiesce to the baby's release for adoption. We certainly felt that there was better than a 50-50 chance that the baby would come home from the hospital with us. It was hard to temper our enthusiasm and optimism with the knowledge that things might yet come apart, and we found our hearts soaring with anticipation of a new family addition.

The next day our hopes began to mount and the passage of time only fueled our eagerness. The morning hours trickled by with no contact. Finally, Abbie called at about 2:00 in the afternoon. Unfortunately, the news was not good; Fred's thinking had not fallen in line as we had expected. On the contrary, he was fighting the release harder than ever. He reportedly ranted to Abbie about how he didn't know if he could trust us after a single meeting. (Interestingly, he had not called Lara's birthmother or taken us up on our invitation for more face-to-face contact.) According to Abbie, he was not being very rational in his thinking. He was even talking about raising the baby himself, and Abbie expressed serious doubts about Fred's ability to parent a newborn at this point in his life. She had warned him that a custody fight might lead Heather to keep the baby and cut him off from all future contact; she suggested that he might have a better ongoing relationship with his son through an open adoption.

The bottom line in all of this was that Heather had decided to take the baby home for a few days in hopes that Fred would come to grips with the realities of the situation during the interim. Heather was anxious for us to see the baby, however, and would be calling us to make arrangements. She had also named the baby at last—Jesse Frederick.

The emotional descent for us was rapid and bruising. We had known that the likelihood of bringing the baby home from the hospital was hardly 100 percent, but that didn't do much to ease the fall. We had let ourselves be swept away by delicious anticipation and now our feelings of disappointment were overwhelming. Heather did call that day to invite us to see the baby on the following afternoon, but while we looked forward to being with Jesse, our longing was accompanied by a healthy dose of apprehension.

Actually, I was beginning to have some serious doubts about going through with the adoption. Could we risk the possibility that Fred would be a persistent problem for the next 18 years? In fact, this situation might present Fred with the kind of motivation necessary to realize an adoptive parent's worst fear—that an irrational birthparent beset by emotion might take the child. If Fred was denied any legal means of getting his son, would he be tempted to do something rash? The more I thought about it, the more I began to believe that we could not expose ourselves to the potential risk, that an open adoption made no sense in *this* situation. While it pained me to think of letting go, I acknowledged that perhaps the baby would have a more secure future in an adoptive home unknown to Fred.

When Jean got home, I told her of my serious misgivings and questioned whether we should press any further. After giving my concerns careful thought, she suggested that it was too early to back out, that perhaps my reassessment of Fred was an over reaction to the emotions of the day. Abbie later gave much the same advice when she talked to Jean on the phone that evening. Abbie did not feel that Fred would do anything out of line if the baby was released, that he could see that it would not be in his son's best interest. Based on this input, I backed off from my pessimistic notions and prepared to give the situation a fresh start in the morning.

By the afternoon of the next day, I was ready to proceed once again. It seemed like an eternity passed before it was time to see Jesse, but finally Jean and Lara and I all went to Heather's parents' home to behold this wondrous child. He *was* beautiful indeed! I held him first and he nestled contentedly in my arms; I was already falling in love with Jesse. As we took turns holding him, it gave us a chance to talk with Heather's mother. Many bridges were built between us that afternoon. I think we were able to offer a lot of reassurance in our willingness to be open and maintain Jesse's biological ties. I think Heather's family sensed our sincerity and Heather's mother told us that she now supported the plan for adoption. It really looked as though the situation was shaping up in many very important ways. We began to feel good about things once again. Seeing that little baby and thinking about taking him into our family certainly made much of the turmoil seem worth enduring.

Before we could even set foot out of the door, our bubble was burst again. Heather received a call from Abbie indicating that Fred was now threatening a custody battle that he could conceivably win. We all stood in disbelief, seeing the amazing potential in our open relationship held at bay by someone who seemingly had little idea of what he was doing. Abbie had scheduled a meeting with Heather and Fred for the following afternoon at 5:00 P.M.; I offered Heather a ride in if she needed it. We left in a somber mood, feeling the foundation of the plan eroding quickly.

From all appearances, the situation looked like it was over for Jean and me. We couldn't allow ourselves to take Jesse home with litigation pending over his custody. There seemed to be no way out short of a miracle. The story was far from its end, however. We were barely home five minutes when Reneé called. She had just spent considerable time talking to Fred on the phone. They had discussed her relationship with us, the quality of our parenting, her level of trust in us, and the degree of openness we shared. She reported that throughout their conversation, Fred had been appropriate and calm.

Within minutes after we hung up the phone, Fred called us. Jean talked with him at length about his feelings and his plans. He said that he had finally accepted adoption as the best alternative for Jesse under the circumstances and he wanted his son released to us. It appeared that at long last, everything was falling into place and that we could finally bring that wonderful little baby boy into our home and hearts. Our spirits really began to soar. Unfortunately, it was a short flight.

Later that night, Jean talked to Abbie on the phone. Her reaction to Fred's sudden change was not what we had expected— "What's he up to now?" She made it clear that she no longer trusted Fred and wondered if he might be using us to manipulate a more favorable court date in front of a visiting judge. Abbie added that both she and Jim Gritter were now wondering if Jean and I should back out so that Jesse could go to a home where his location could be kept a guarded secret.

The descent was ever more rapid; the fall was crushing. Just as our hearts were flying toward an emotional pinnacle, everything seemed to be coming apart. I couldn't take the sudden reversals anymore. I wanted it to end—*now!* I was angry—why had I let people talk me out of my pessimistic assessment on the previous day; I was *ready* to get out then. But now it was so much harder—I *had seen the baby!* It would have been so much easier to walk away before I had seen and held Jesse; now it was much more painful. Escape! I wanted and needed escape from this whole situation. It is unusual for me to have trouble sleeping, but I slept a total of three hours that night. Poor Jean, she not only had to deal with her own sense of loss and disappointment, but with my extreme anger and sadness over what had happened.

By the next morning I was about ready to accept the fact that it was over. Yet, somehow the brief time I had spent with Jesse kept me clinging to a small glimmer of hope that everything could still be magically resolved. For the most part I had resigned myself to reality, but I left the door open just the barest crack. I really didn't think we'd hear any more from either Heather or Fred; I thought that the agency would simply explain to them that an open arrangement could no longer be supported and that would be the end of it for us.

Once more I was wrong, with the phone again shattering the silence. It was Heather; apparently unaware of what had transpired, she was requesting the ride I offered. This caught me completely off guard; I didn't know how to respond. What was the point in following through with my offer, wasn't the situation hopeless? I felt empty inside. Something—I don't know what—drove me to tell her I would pick her up.

The ride into Traverse City was difficult for me, but I tried to look at it as an opportunity to set the stage for what was likely to come. In my conversation with Heather, while I played along as though little had changed, I also made a point to express that Jean and I were prepared to bow out gracefully if that was ultimately in Jesse's best interests. Heather let me know loud and clear that she did not want us to "bow out", that she still wanted to release her baby to us. It was frustrating seeing such a potentially good relationship develop between us and knowing that it would probably all be for naught.

After I dropped Heather off at the agency, I met Jean at a local restaurant. Jean had made arrangements for us to meet with Abbie after Heather and Fred's appointment, and we tried to prepare ourselves for what seemed the inevitable conclusion. While I still hung on to a thread of hope, Jean had virtually none. Little did we suspect that the wheel of fortune was about to quickly shift another 180 degrees.

When we got to the agency, Abbie explained some new developments. A probate court date had miraculously opened up for the next day. She proposed having both Fred and Heather terminate their parental rights at the hearing and turn the baby over to us immediately thereafter. Not only was Fred willing to go along with this plan, he heartily endorsed it. Abbie tried to get them to look at other adoptive couples to make sure that they were really content with their decision; neither of them wanted to consider anybody else—they wanted us!

Fred came out to talk to us and told us how difficult it was for him to terminate his parental rights. He said that he knew, however, that adoption would be the best plan and he was confident that we would take good care of Jesse. The sudden turnaround of events left us literally dumbfounded.

After Fred left, we tried to get Abbie's best assessment of Fred's intentions. From all she could see, they were honorable. She felt that, if the hearing went off as planned, Fred would not be a problem. Based on this, we resolved that we would give the release one last shot. If parental rights were terminated, we would gladly proceed with the adoption; if anything went wrong, we had already had all of the heartbreak we could stand and we would have to pass on the adoption. The hearing was set for 2:00 P.M. the following day; Abbie would call us immediately afterward to apprise us of the status.

We awakened the next morning believing that there would be a new addition to our household by nightfall. We knew that there was still some slim chance that Fred would 'flip-flop' again, but it really appeared as though everyone was finally working together. Our spirits were high once more. Alone at home, I floated around getting things in order; I definitely wanted to be ready if Abbie gave us the go-ahead.

At about noon, the phone rang; it was Fred. Something rather unexpected was about to throw a wrench in our plans again. He said that Heather did not feel she could go through with the scheduled court hearing. My heart sank, my mind raced. I suggested that Fred keep his 1:00 P.M. appointment with Abbie, and I would see if I could reach Abbie for some timely intervention with Heather. It took almost an hour to link up with Abbie on the phone. After hearing of the latest developments, she said that she would call back as soon as she had some definite word—there was still time to try to get Heather into court by two o'clock. I called Jean to fill her in, then waited by the telephone.

One hour passed, then another. I braced myself for bad news. At about 3:30 P.M. it came when Abbie finally called. She said that Heather could not go through with the hearing despite the pleading of Fred that she do so. Heather complained of feeling too much pressure, of feeling overwhelmed by it all. She was confused and didn't know what she wanted to do.

That was it! I simply couldn't take any more. I had reached the limits of my emotional flexibility. I told Abbie that while I wouldn't absolutely rule out the possibility of some eleventh-hour plan, we would be withdrawing ourselves from consideration for this adoption. The baby had been held out to us like the carrot-on-a-stick one too many times. I reassured her that our faith in the program had not been shaken one iota, that I knew that this situation had been *unusually* difficult. I also asked that our file be reactivated immediately for consideration by other birthparents. We tried to offer each other support and it was apparent that we were both in tears by the end of the conversation.

I called Jean to give her the latest news. She seemed to take it better than I had, perhaps she was already steeled for the worst. Then my entire emotional system collapsed. Tears poured from me in sobs; I ached to the very core. It was more than an hour before I was able to pull myself together.

The ominous phone rang again. What could it be now; who wanted to break my heart this time? Unbelievably, it was Fred. He had spent the afternoon talking with Heather. She still wanted to go through with the release. They wanted to talk with Jean and me to see if there was some way we might consider giving it one more try. I told them that we would probably meet with them, but they needed to understand how emotionally bruising the week had been for us and appreciate how hard it would be for us to subject ourselves to further risk. I said that I would talk to Jean when she got home and get back with them.

To say the least, Jean was reluctant to go any further. It was only at my urging that she agreed to meet with Fred and Heather one more time. Somehow I sensed some reason for hope, it seemed like Fred and Heather truly wanted to make it work. I felt that the possibility of bringing Jesse home made this final risk worth taking.

Heather and Fred came over early that evening. Heather wanted to explain why she did not keep the court date and expressed how the sudden request for termination of rights had overwhelmed her. She found that she just couldn't handle all of the family dynamics and external pressure with so little time and preparation. She stressed that she had *not* changed her mind about the release and that she still wanted Jesse to live with us. Her explanation seemed reasonable. Fred confirmed that he was equally committed to making the adoption work.

Jean asked them what specific plan they had in mind. Fred said that he wanted to bring the baby home for two days to allow his family some time with him. He suggested that he pick the baby up from Heather's house on Friday and that Jesse be released to us on Sunday morning at his parents' home. I was a little reluctant to accept anything short of an immediate release, but Jean quickly saw the wisdom in their plan. She urged that they take the next few days to entertain any second thoughts they might have and that they shouldn't release the baby to us unless they were absolutely committed to it. She pointed out that it would be far easier for us to accept and cope with a change in heart *before* the baby came to our home then afterward. This was the plan we all endorsed that night.

The next few days were a little tense and we tried to keep any optimism in check. We wanted to be prepared if the whole arrangement collapsed once again; we wanted to minimize the potential for pain. When Sunday came, our feelings of anticipation were beginning to swell and we felt ourselves hurtling toward an unknown climax. Finally, at 11 A.M., Fred called. He said that they wanted us to come and get Jesse. Jean questioned once again if they were absolutely sure that they wanted to go ahead; she asked if they wanted a few more days to think things over. Fred said that they wanted to proceed *now*. We packed ourselves in the car and left, having little idea what kind of reception awaited us.

We were relieved to find Fred's family very warm and supportive. They really tried to make us feel comfortable. We talked with them about openness and told them that they were welcome in our home whenever they felt the need to see Jesse. While it was obviously a difficult day for everyone, you could feel all of us pulling together to make the plan work. Finally, when it came time to leave, the tears began to flow. There were heartfelt hugs all around. Embracing Heather, I thanked her for trusting us. Then

I looked at Fred's mother and said, "We're all family now." Just as we had after Lara's release, we left feeling less than joyous. We were certainly pleased to bring Jesse into our home, but it takes a while to shake the sadness and pain you have just shared with the birthfamily. It is something you never forget.

Over the next few days, we spent a lot of extra time bonding with Jesse, perhaps trying to make up for the time we had lost in the first eight days of his life. He soon settled in and seemed very content in his new surroundings. We sure fell in love with him quickly. As he looked up with his sweet, innocent eyes, it was scary to think how close we had come to giving up. Our perseverance and willingness to accept risks had certainly paid off. We were glad that we had gone the extra mile when it had been extraordinarily difficult to do so. Without a doubt, taking this beautiful little boy into our family was well worth our walk through emotional fire.

The phone rang. Jesse had been with us three days now and I had just wrapped him up in a towel after giving him his bath. It was Abbie; there were some new developments. Jean got on the extension. As Jesse looked up at me with all of the sweetness and contentment he could muster, Abbie informed us that Fred had changed his mind again; he had gotten an attorney and was planning to sue for custody.

It was over—finally, once and for all—it was over! There was no more thinking to do, no more glimmer of hope, no possibilities of an eleventh-hour rescue, no last minute pleas for reconsideration—no way to keep Jesse in our family. We could not allow ourselves to face months of litigation over custody on the slim chance that everything would magically work out. Even if Fred changed his mind about legal action, he had reversed himself so many times that we could no longer trust that he wouldn't do it again. The only rational course was to let go, pick up the pieces, and move on.

From the agency's perspective, Abbie and Jim didn't see how they could possibly let us go any further. Surprisingly, there was some comfort in the finality of it all—there would be no more sudden twists and turns to cause us pain. After talking with Abbie, we decided to return Jesse to the agency on the following morning so that he could be placed in temporary foster care.

I don't know where I found the strength to get through the night as well as I did. Maybe it was knowing that Jesse needed that strength, that he had to be protected from the tension and pain. There were no tears this time, only a begrudging acceptance. Throughout the night I gave Jesse the same loving care I had before, and in return I got the same gazes of contentment. It was far more difficult for Jean—those sweet little eyes were all too haunting for her. We struggled on; there was a lot to think about and reflect upon.

Although this situation had been emotionally bruising from start to finish, neither of us lost faith with the essential wisdom of openness. Yes, we had been one of the families who was hurt in the process, but we knew the pain would be temporary and that the program's potential for enormously positive outcomes made it worth the risk. When we thought back on our experience with Lara's birth—being at the hospital when she was born, bonding with her from her earliest moments, taking her home from the hospital, enjoying a wonderful relationship with her birthmother's family—it was clear that the program's benefits far outweighed the pain we had just suffered. While we would never forget Jesse and how he touched our lives , while we would always care and wonder about his well-being, it was comforting to know that there would be another baby for us sometime in the future and that a more promising end was likely.

Now, a month after we released Jesse, I am surprised at how quickly we have bounced back. I am sure that having one child at home helped a great deal. Things are now pretty much as they were before and our thoughts of Jesse center more on what a beautiful little boy he was rather than on any losses we suffered.

The whole experience has given us one other important piece of insight. Some people might assert that it isn't fair to expect adoptive parents to deal with the pain of separation when a placement fails to work out. Our reaction, however, was quite the opposite. How eminently fair it is, when adoptive parents derive the joy of parenthood from someone else's loss, that they be willing to release a baby themselves when the situation demands. It is an ironic form of justice that some adoptive parents are called upon to make such a sacrifice. After spending four days bonding with Jesse, we had to wonder if our pain even minimally compared to what birthparents must feel when it is their time to let go.

I will certainly never forget the morning we released Jesse. We got up and got everybody ready to go. We decided that Jean would take Lara to her grandma's house and we would meet at the agency. Somehow I still remained strong—right up until it was time to put Jesse in the car. It was then that the grief struck me and the tears came. I managed to regain my composure by the time we got to town, and Jean and I solemnly carried Jesse and his belongings into the building.

We spent about an hour and a half with Abbie, holding the baby and talking about our feelings. Finally, it was time to go. The tears came again. Jean held the baby one last time as the grief swept over us. Then I took him. I squeezed him tightly trying to express all of the love I felt for him in that final embrace. Tearfully, I gave him to Abbie and said my last goodbye. The words almost stuck in my throat as I tried to choke back the sobs, "Grow so big, little guy, grow so big."

Mary and Gary Joslin

"A sense of completeness for everyone"

Our adoptive experience has been one of great joy, vulnerability, and sensibility. So much is questioned in adoption—our values, our attitudes, our ability to parent, even our ability to love. We realized all along that there was a tremendous concern for children at the heart of all this inquiry, but sometimes it can be almost overpowering. Some of this is endemic to the adoption experience, for it is undeniably an unnatural means of fashioning a family. We both believe open adoption can, and in fact for us did, make the experience seem more natural.

Adopted myself in the fifties, I had strong convictions that our children must encounter no closed doors or secrets. As a social worker trained in therapy and issues of personality development, I knew that fantasy and unresolved identity issues can powerfully undermine a young person's sense of meaningfulness. I was convinced from both personal and professional experience that children and adults can deal far better with what is known than they can with the unknown.

At the time of our adoption I was working in a private family service agency not too unlike Community, Family and Children Services. It was different in that its adoption program was largely a closed system. I was working with foster children and recognized that even with their fragmented and disrupted backgrounds, the children retained an interest in and a sense of connectedness to their birthfamilies. I also saw that this desire for connectedness did not typically interfere with the willingness of the children to join a more fully prepared family. This helped me overcome any possessive fears I may have had about sharing our baby with his or her birthfamily. My husband, Gary, a self-employed businessman, found it simple to accept the prospect of open adoption. Because he thoroughly enjoys people, he was pleased that openness would enable him to add to the number of important people in his life.

It was 10:00 P.M. on a Tuesday night when Jim Gritter called. Gary answered the phone. I could tell from the excitement in his voice when he called out "Mary!" that this was not a run-of-the-mill phone call. Jim explained that a young birthcouple was interested in meeting us and wondered if we could come down the next morning. The baby had been born on Sunday, and the next morning one of the Detroit newspapers had featured a full-page article on the agency's adoption program. Two different people had brought the article to Brenda and Jeff's attention and since they had not finalized arrangements with any other agency, they decided to contact Community, Family and Children Services.

To everyone's good fortune, there was a break in Jim's schedule and he was able to get there the next day. Comforted to have made contact, Brenda left the hospital although the baby remained there while a plan was formulated.

Jim spent most of Tuesday with Brenda and Jeff getting to know and understand them and their motivation for adoption. They were only juniors in high school, but they were both exceptionally mature in their thinking. Once Jim was convinced that they had considered all their alternatives and that their plan was not impulsive or ill-conceived, he agreed to move into the selection process. They poured over a number of prospective adoptive parents and ultimately chose us! Jim later explained that it was very unusual for plans to come together so quickly, and that he only felt free to do that because of Brenda and Jeff's exceptional stability and sincerity. We interpreted the swiftness with which all the loose ends came together as an indication that we were all truly meant for each other. If any of the timing had been the least bit different, we might never have gotten to know each other.

Gary and I made arrangements that evening to miss work the next day and began to psychologically prepare ourselves for a baby. We had a meager 14 hours to get ready, and the only supply we had laid in was a teddy bear. Neither of us could sleep, so at four o'clock in the morning we went out to view Halley's Comet. Although the comet is widely regarded as an astronomical extravaganza, it seemed a little pale compared to the excitement in our lives and it could not hold our attention. We decided to head for Detroit.

We arrived much too early and began to drive around aimlessly to kill a little time. Our conversation was completely disjointed and off the wall. We were tired and we were exhilarated. Finally the appointed hour arrived and we drove to the home of Brenda's parents.

Our meeting with Brenda and Jeff was emotional, difficult, and somehow surreal. In our earlier excitement we had failed to grasp the fact that the baby was still in the hospital, so we kept expecting to hear or see the baby. Finally I asked with poorly disguised confusion, "Where's the baby?" It was a relief to get that clarified, and my powers of concentration improved.

Another issue I was unclear about was whether Brenda and Jeff had settled on us or whether they were simply interviewing us. That drama gradually dissipated as it became evident that we had met their approval. Next we turned our attention to names. They had named the baby Stephan. We proposed a slight modification to Steven and that important process was settled. Finally our collective energy shifted to Steven and plans for his discharge from the hospital.

At the hospital our emotions ranged from elation and almost delirious excitement to great sadness for the anguish Brenda and Jeff were experiencing. The hospital social worker seemed very unsure of this type of adoption and was dotting every "i" and crossing every "t." Jim later noted that such behavior was not uncommon, since open adoption is relatively new and has many detractors. One moment, as we neared the time of discharge, encapsulated the awkwardness at the hospital perfectly. The nurse wanted me to sit in the wheelchair and be wheeled out holding Steven. I much preferred that Brenda have this honor, but felt paralyzed to say anything. I was greatly relieved when Jim intervened and suggested that Brenda be wheeled out with the baby.

We were all in tears as we drove away and it seemed as though we were kidnapping their child. I already felt connected to Brenda and sensed her desperation as we left them. They were leaving for Boston for their junior class trip on Friday, a fact which somewhat disconcerted me. I wanted them closer so I could protect them. I became aware of my maternal feelings for Brenda, feelings which continue even today. She was so young, so strong, but also so determined to do what she felt was right. At sixteen she had faced a very difficult time in her life with a grace and maturity far beyond her years.

We felt secure in our relationship with Brenda and Jeff from the very beginning. We knew that they and their families were honest people and that our interactions with them would always be caring and straightforward. While there was some anxiety while we waited for their court hearing to occur—a time during which either one of them could change course—it was never more than a flicker. When the court day arrived, Brenda and Jeff were accompanied by all four parents. With the hearing over, they came to our house for a visit. While it was difficult at first, both Brenda and her mother later commented that it comforted them to see us interact with Steven in our home. From our perspective, it was enlightening to observe the many ways Steven resembled the two families. To the delight of us all, the more we talked, the more similarities we discovered. We are all people interested in running, skiing, and other participatory sports. Since Gary's family had owned a car dealership for many years, he was interested to learn that both birthgrandfathers are employed in auto-related businesses. The numerous commonalities served to cement our sense of compatibility.

I know from my own experience how difficult growing up is when questions are asked for which there are no answers. I distinctly remember feeling painfully embarrassed when my mother was asked some medical question at the doctor's office and the quiet response when she explained that she didn't know since I was adopted. I always felt different in the "odd" sense of the word and am relieved and pleased that I can answer so many more questions in Steven's behalf. What's more, if I don't know an answer, it is only a phone call away.

Our relationship since has been good, although contact has been less frequent than we would like. Usually I renew contact with letters, pictures, and occasional phone calls. Brenda and Jeff have visited three times over the last year and the visits have all gone well. They are both in college now and seem to be getting on with their lives very well. Jeff has decided at this time to back off from our relationship. Although we are sad about this, we understand and accept his position. Brenda does want to keep in touch, and as she moves through life, Gary and I watch from afar with something akin to pride.

What was important and central to our adoptive experience was the sense of completeness for everyone involved. Our son will know a great deal about his birth heritage and will have a relationship with his birthfamily if he so chooses. His birthparents seem comfortable and free to press on with life because they know us and know they will be kept apprised of developments in Steven's life.

Open adoption is a fluid arrangement which can grow and evolve with the changes in our lives. It feels as natural as birth and life itself. We take pleasure in being part of the transformation of adoption from something austere and incomplete to something warm and natural.

Tom and Sue Bohnhorst

"A lock of Brendan's hair"

Eastward we flew. Down that long lonesome highway to nearby Traverse City. We had two appointments to keep, my wife Sue and I. We didn't talk much. I said it often—"It'll be fine . . . it'll be fine . . ."— but mostly I just squeezed the fingerholds on the steering wheel and wondered how to control the stomach flutters which lifted to tingles beneath my scalp. And of course I had the luxury of meditating on the highway's middle lines, racing by like the poundings of my heart.

We would go along for several silent minutes until Sue would start up again. "Oh my, Tom! Oh my, my!"

"It'll be fine," I said and squeezed the steering wheel tight.

This was early October when the first crimson leaves held the promise of certain change, but when most trees still clung to the green of summer.

Nature insists that healthy pregnancies require the duration of seasons, of a certain number of months and weeks. And the irony occurred to me as we cruised along that it had been nearly nine months to the day since Sue and I had walked into our first orientation meeting at the adoption agency. Yes, on Friday, just three days earlier and nine months since that original meeting, Jim called from the agency to say that, well, he had talked to a certain person, and well, things had come together in a hurry and well . . .

"Jim, should I be sitting down?" I asked.

I sat down as he directed. Jim began the story of Robin, a 17-year-old who gave birth to a baby boy three months earlier, and . . .

"A boy?" I whispered. "A baby boy?"

I tried hard to hang with Jim's every word as he told the story of this baby boy's topsy-turvy existence thus far. But I was intermittently overcome by stomach flutters as Jim's earlier words of wonder swept through my being: "A boy . . . A baby boy . . . "

I did gather the essence of the brief history which would soon be delivered into our lives. Jim explained that Robin had had her share of adolescent upheaval—a turbulent relationship at home, bumps and scrapes with drinking and drugs, hot and heavy relationships with boys. When she found out she was pregnant, Robin voluntarily entered the agency's substance abuse counseling program and remained drug free for the full term. This was how she became involved with the agency's teen-parent services, and thus familiar with the adoption services—and with Sue and me.

Robin named the baby Brandon Gene, and she had every intention of keeping Brandon Gene after delivery though she had long since broken off her relationship with the father. But life remained extremely rocky on the home front, and the prospects for Robin's retaining custody of the baby were shaky in light of this. Robin and Robin's mother suffered the worst of storms with one another, and Brandon Gene was placed in foster care on two separate occasions as Robin simply could not find a proper answer out in the tough foreign world on her own. Throughout, Robin continued to receive counseling from the agency, and she finally decided that the right thing would be to place Brandon Gene with an adoptive couple.

Jim had introduced Robin to the application files of several likely candidates, and Robin especially liked what she saw in us. Could Sue and I come to Traverse City on Monday, just three days later, to meet with Robin and later to see the baby? Robin had changed her mind about a lot of things of late, said Jim, but this was something she was 100 percent set on doing. So could we come on Monday to get the show on the road?

Could we!

Nine months seems like a fine design in preparing a parent for the onslaught. But also by design, most adoptive parents must somehow cram nine months' emotional anticipation onto the cluttered terrain of just a few peculiar moments and a few peculiar days. After Jim's call, when I had finally gathered the coordination to walk, I yanked Sue out of her fifth-grade classroom and presented her with a card.

"It's a boy," she read. From eyes, to pies, to moons, to the Fourth of July, to cheeks streamed with tears.

"Oh my, Tom!" she cried, "Oh my, my!"

We idled at the light at Chum's Corners, only ten minutes now from our meeting with Robin. "It'll be fine," I consoled when I heard my wife moan. But as we accelerated away, Sue dropped her forehead to her knee. "Who-uh! . . . who-uh! . . . who-uh!" I stroked her back as I pointed the car north. Good grief . . . the dry heaves.

For Sue, this was one of those peculiar moments when the anticipation compacted itself so tightly that her stomach thought its inside was out. But this little moment stood in sharp contrast to our behavior during the weekend's preparation. My wife should have attached a lead rope to my wrist as I literally followed her from store to store in the process of building our nest. There was absolutely no response I could offer to her suggestions and questions; I would lend a serious look, a grit of my teeth, and finally a defeated shake of my head. I marveled at the sheer industry and organization of my seemingly omniscient wife as she piled the diapers, mattress pads, butt wipes, crib bumpers, shirts, overalls, squeezie things, and so on into the shopping cart. Well, there was absolutely nothing I could offer until I saw the cap. My son would wear this cap—this blue corduroy cap with a slight brim, a blue corduroy strap, a button on the top, and best of all, the little yellow and red feather stuck in the side—a feather that said "I like to cruise, and I like to cruise in style."

Back at home, Sue motored around, occasionally soliciting my thoughts, busying herself to make ready. I usually watched the hubbub from a safe distance—can a turnip assist Einstein?—and found myself losing ground in a never-never land of anxiety. So on Sunday I groped to find some use for this torrent of nervous energy which seemed destined to erupt in some dastardly way. I headed out the door, tennis racket and balls in hand. The thwack, thwack, thwack of the balls slamming against a backboard just might be the only therapeutic backtalk that could make any sense of it all, that might give cadence to my wild heart.

Thwack! The obnoxious monotony sent me back nine months when Sue and I first walked into the agency's orientation meeting for prospective adoptive parents. Jim sat cross-ankled atop a table and steered this group of twenty around the pillars which form the structure of the "openness" approach. He kept harping about birthmothers. He spoke about their love for their infants, and the selfless courage and integrity required to relinquish. He talked about adoptees who searched, sometimes for lifetimes, for birthparents who seemed forever locked away by the traditional practice of secrecy. He stated at the beginning, and at the end, that open adoption was not for everyone.

Thwack! My errant tennis ball sailed over the fence, down the hill, and into the ravine. As I lazily swatted the ferns, I recalled the meeting at the traditional agency across town. Had we signed on with them, Sue and I would have been ever so slowly climbing rungs. We would not be meeting with a stranger named Robin tomorrow, but would be awaiting our number to be called when we reached the top of the ladder, much like customers awaiting their numbers in a store. No, despite the overwhelming apprehension attached to our meetings the next day, it felt right . . . it felt right. I swatted a fern again—no ball. There was another one in the can.

Thwack! I am passing the ball with a little more pace now, working up a sweat, finding the sweet spot again and again. At that first meeting, Jim said a thing which made me shift my weight: "In working through our adoption practices, we place the interests of the child first; the interests of the birthparents second; and the interests of the adoptive parents third." Sue and I began to see ourselves as a future point on a fragile and extraordinary triangle, a position which reached out in two separate directions, and a position which carried two sets of responsibilities. And tomorrow—oh sweet mystery of tomorrow—tomorrow the flesh and blood reality of our triangle will be made a creation! And it felt right, so uncompromisingly right, because . . . now I knew! Robin, sweet stranger and birthmother to our son, Robin made a choice. Robin chose us! Robin chose us to be parents to her son!

Thwack! Thwack! Thwack! Jimmy Conners would have been on his knees from the blur of my passing groundstrokes.

Just in time, Sue's stomach found peace as we came to rest in the agency parking lot. No doubt we had a look of cool nonchalance as we took seats outside Jim's office where we awaited a rendezvous that would forever change our lives. We sat quietly, our eyes peering at the pages of magazines whose messages we could not then comprehend. I was lost in a fantasy world of expectation. And in my "most likely scenario," I pictured a meek and mild Robin taking her seat in a room full of adults, embarrassed by the attention she had brought herself, maintaining her thread of composure, yet anxious for the end so that the ordeal might be done forever. I suppose this was my "safe" scenario, and I promised myself I would be a model of compassion, full of courtesy and warmth. I glanced over at Sue, and she grabbed my eyes with her own, arching her eyebrows in a look that said simply, "I cannot believe this is happening . . . I cannot believe . . . " Sue's "most likely scenario" was apparently marooned by a fearful case of the heebie-jeebies.

Jim finally escorted us to his office where we would shortly meet with Robin. We asked about the baby, how he was, where he was, and Jim said that Abbie, the agency's teen-parent worker, would take us to a church office after our meeting with Robin. That was where his foster mother worked and the baby would be there to greet us.

And then Robin entered. Accompanied by Abbie, she shook our hands with a gutsy strength, and as she took her seat before us, my little fantasy of the meek and mild went howling out of sight. Robin took quick command of the conversation, engineering an exchange that was polite, humorous, and dramatically sincere. Here was an attractive, articulate woman-child, eager to learn the simple facts of our lives, eager to convey the history and habits of our baby-to-be. She liked the fact that we were educators, artistically and creatively inclined, that we lived in a rural-small town setting, that our extended families were solid and strong, that we conveyed warmth in manner, She told us of the baby's father, that they had had a wonderful relationship, until for unknown reasons it became sexually centered, that communication between them had ceased. He was entirely out of the picture now, she explained, though she told us of his appearance, his interests. She eagerly told us of her plans to carry out her goals of education. She told us of her struggle with alcohol, but she did so without a hint of despair, as though she were en route to customary success once this hazard was forcefully tamed.

I was astounded. Not because the circumstances were astounding, which indeed they were. I was astounded by the girl—the quick wit, the quick grin, the eager-to-please, the come-what-may, the brighter tomorrow, the somewhat exaggerated talk. I was astounded by the woman—the hard knocks, the developed street smarts, the sacrificial decisions, the bigger perspectives, the charm and beauty, the outward confidence.

It seemed as though Jim was keen on observing Sue and me throughout the meeting, and when I was reeling with astonishment at this small creature, Jim's eyes met mine. I shook my head from wonder, and he smiled at me as if to say, "Ain't this just grand!" Well, it was that and a whole lot more, though Sue and I have yet to be able to put the words on it.

Robin was the one to set forth the shape of things to come. She said the last thing she wanted was to "interfere." She said she knew that many birthmothers continued friendships and on-going contacts with adoptive families, but she thought it best to leave what she knew was well enough alone. Robin had but one request: She asked if someday we would send her a lock of Brandon's hair.

This was a bittersweet moment, and Sue took charge of our promises to keep. We would of course send her a lock of hair, and we would send her birthday messages, and Christmas greetings, and pictures, and tales of his accomplishments. And Sue asked if Robin would one day write him a letter, so that he might have a more complete and healthy understanding of the events he would never remember, but would assuredly ponder time and time again. Robin enthusiastically agreed to do this, of course, and we agreed to channel our correspondences through the agency.

Shortly before departing, Robin was anxious to learn what name we had chosen for her birthson. It was my turn to take charge. Sue and I had flipped through the names on the pages of some "Name That Baby" books, I explained, and no suggestion could alter our original choice. The child was some days beyond the age of three months, so the name "Brandon" had tagged along with him for quite some time. We liked "Brandon," but we liked a similar name quite a bit more. Sue and I decided on this new name out of respect for the original, and because he is our son, we want him to have one that we, his parents, have chosen. That is why his name will be similar, and that is why his name will be different. He will now be called "Brendan."

What's in a name? Robin was visibly moved by this little bit of information, and like a tangible lock of hair or a picture from his tenth birthday party, Brendan's name will no doubt stand forever as an important link for her, for us, for him. But this choice of name was not a gift to Robin. It was the right and proper dubbing for one so dear to all of us.

She left with that gutsy handshake, full of smiles. There was no doubt that Robin had long endured the company of tears, but now she seemed full of peace and happiness that she had made the best choice. And no doubt she would endure many more long moments, but I will always remember that wonderful smile before she walked out the door.

Abbie accompanied Robin away, and soon returned, her eyes moistened and her face agrin from the touching and glorious meeting we had had. It was now Abbie's happy task to take us to Brendan. And off we went after strong pats on the back with Jim.

The short ride over lacked the sweet horror we had known a few hours earlier. No "safe scenarios," no dry heaves. Abbie talked freely of her admiration for Robin, and Sue and I felt, well, as though we were on some wondrous crescendo of awe. Let us feast our eyes on him . . . let us hold him.

We walked down the short corridor to the room where he lay napping. Brendan's kind and gentle foster mother roused him and held him to her shoulder, where Sue and I could at once come face to face with him. He protested a moment, then focused his eyes on a pair of strangers who could barely contain themselves for what they now saw. Sprouts of bright white hair above the neck, little pug nose, giant blinks from sleepy eyes, perfect baby features which sent genetic messages of Robin, and like a cliché, he flashed his proud father a gummy grin . . .

Perhaps here is where "the extraordinary" of our adoption experience those short years ago might end. Because it was then that we shared the universal joy of all new parents—the touch, the immediate sealing of bonds, the soul-driven commitment to part the earth's seas, if need be, to make the way safe. Here is where we stepped into a Relationship of which we had dreamed for years.

We brought him home the next day. As we wheeled westward, I selfishly wished Sue had driven so that I could be the one to just stare and stare into that sleeping face aboard the safety seat in the front. We found a "Welcome Home Brendan" banner strewn across our dining room, affixed by friends who would soon be joining us. And Sue watched as I gave him the guided tour—he was introduced to his crib, our collie named "Lad," the kitchen sink, the wood stove, and a squeezie thing or two.

Then it was time: "Let's see how you look," I cooed. Atop his head I placed a cap, a blue corduroy cap replete with a button, blue corduroy strap, and a most dignified feather of yellow and red. "You look like you're gonna cruise," I said. "Brendan, my little dude, you're gonna cruise in style."

Since these meetings in 1983, we have kept our promises with Robin, and she with us. We hear that she stops in at the agency from time to time, eager for any information of Brendan, and we are happy to send some news her way, in addition to our Christmas and birthday greetings. We are also eager to learn of her latest adventures. As of the last word, she's doing well . . . we are all doing well.

Is this an "open" adoption? Not really. Is this a "closed" adoption? No. But there are two aspects of our story which seem identical to all the other stories we've heard which have been engendered from the "openness" approach. The first is that we, the players in this extraordinary adventure, are left free and open to make choices *with* one another, *for* one another. And each of these newly formed relationships with birthparents is unique, as unique as the players themselves. Openness comes from the free and common choices in forming the most appropriate relationships for the adoptee.

The second common denominator in our adoption experience stems from our openness approach with Brendan. We have been calmly matter-of-fact with him when discussing his roots. We have not "chosen a best moment" to "unload the bombshell." We have been open from the outset, and before Brendan reached the age of three, he was full of questions about his birthmother, how he was born, why she relinquished, what she looked like. We have thanked our lucky stars that we had that indispensable meeting with Robin so that we could provide him the ready answers, quickly and honestly. I cannot imagine the experience of our adoption without that meeting with Robin. And as Brendan brings forth future questions, we hope he will do so partly because we have been open with him, and have the answers at hand.

I often see Robin in Brendan's face, her radiant charm in wishing us the best. This is a great comfort for us. And one day he might have the honor of seeing her again. Why would we ever deny him that?

And something says that our meeting with Robin brought home the greatest gift of all. Perhaps the meeting was a gigantic leap in allowing her to become whole again.

Mary and Rick Rybicki

"The truth is easier . . . "

If you ask our daughter Rachel, age four, how it feels to be adopted, she'll answer in one word: "Great!" We'd like to think her positive feelings on being adopted are due, at least in part, to the "open adoption" experience.

When we were first introduced to the concept of open adoption by CFCS at our orientation meeting in March of 1981, we felt very comfortable. No one had to "talk us into it." Open adoption made sense to us because the truth is easier to deal with than a bunch of unknowns. Also, we were curious to know all there is to know about our child in order to share this information with her. And when you love someone, don't you want to get to know everything about them? Well, our children's birthparents are so much a part of our children that we wanted to know them, too.

So ends the lecture on how we got into open adoption and why we are so comfortable with it.

We have been fortunate enough to have had *four* experiences with open adoption, each one a little different and each one teaching us more about ourselves and others.

Rachel

The first time we saw our daughter Rachel, she was with Mrs. Popp, her foster mom, at K-Mart. Carol Popp is one of those remarkable people with a limitless capacity for loving and nurturing children. Nestled comfortably in a hip sling, Rachel was about ten weeks old and had a snotty nose. It's funny the things you remember. At the time we saw her, we knew through the grapevine just a little bit about her: mainly, that she was in foster care and was probably going to be adopted. When I spoke to Jim the next day or so, I mentioned seeing Rachel and said, "It's too bad she hasn't been placed in an adoptive home yet, since the older she gets, the harder it'll be for her to adjust." I guess Jim took this as a sign that we were interested, because he called later that day to ask if we'd like to come to the agency the next morning to talk about adopting Rachel.

At our meeting the next morning, Jim explained that Rachel's birthmother wanted to release her for adoption but Luis, her birthfather, was fighting for her custody. Jim thought more likely than not Rachel would be released to an adoptive home, but the court date was almost a month away. Would we want to take the chance this would all work out and take her home in a couple of days? We picked Rachel up from the foster mom's home two days later. Even though we had seen her a week before in K-Mart, we felt like we were seeing her for the first time because now she was *our* daughter. Naturally, we thought she was the most beautiful baby we'd ever seen. Rick thought she was so smart because she knew how to burp. I hated to tell him burping is a standard feature of all babies.

Jim called in late September to tell us that Luis had given up the fight for Rachel's custody. We were so relieved. We met Luis at the agency in October. Jim asked him why he had decided to give up the fight for Rachel's custody. Luis said he'd gone hunting and, while out in the woods, had time to think. He realized, at this time, that he couldn't offer Rachel much; he had no job, no place of his own. But he did love her, and he always would.

Luis talked about how bad his mother, Mary, felt that he gave up the fight for Rachel's custody. We offered to take Rachel to see his mom the next weekend. I'm sure we made a good first impression—we went to the wrong house, so Mary's neighbor got to see Rachel before she did. Mary cried when she held Rachel.

We tried to reassure her that this was not a one-time visit; we planned to stay in contact.

Over the past four years, we have all gotten together every couple of months, at Mary's house, ours, or Luis'. We've gotten together to celebrate birthdays, Christmas, Easter, and just to play euchre and visit. Rachel really enjoys spending time with "Papa Luis." We know Rachel is a part of their family; they have made us feel that we are, too.

Elizabeth

After we had had Rachel for a year or so, we began to think about adopting another child. We knew there would always be enough couples in line to take babies; we felt maybe we should consider adopting an older child the second time around. So with this in mind, we went to an orientation meeting in December, 1983. At the meeting, they called this the "Special Needs Group." Less than a year later we found out why.

We had moved up to the Petoskey area for Rick's job in the fall of 1984. We were settled there a whole six weeks when I got a call from Jim. Jim said he had a three-week-old baby girl to tell us about. The foster family (the same family that had had Rachel) were calling her Linda. She was born with Turner's Syndrome, which meant she was missing an "x" chromosome. One side-effect of Turner's Syndrome was a heart problem, for which she had had surgery already. Also, she would be very short and would have to take hormones at puberty. Jim encouraged me to talk it over with Rick, but we both knew that was just a formality. When Rick got home that night, he said, "Whatever you think."

I called Jim back and we decided to see the baby on Friday, when we were going to Traverse City anyway. By the time Thursday rolled around, we knew we were going to take the baby, so Jim said, "Why make two trips?"—we could just take her home on Friday. (Here's a little something I'm sure even Jim doesn't know: On Thursday night I talked to someone—who will remain anonymous—who let it slip that *maybe* the baby was retarded, in addition to all her other health problems. When I told Rick this on Thursday night, he said, "She'll fit right in here, won't she?"

When we picked Elizabeth up we couldn't believe how tiny she was. We decided on the name Elizabeth because that's what the Popps had called Rachel while they had her, and we liked the name. I had some questions about caring for her but Mrs. Popp assured me the doctors told her to treat Elizabeth like any other newborn. Only Elizabeth wasn't like any other newborn; she only took an ounce at a time, so she needed to be fed every hour and a half to two hours around the clock. She had a tiny little face. We called her "munchkin."

Her birthmom, Gretchen, called us after we'd had Elizabeth about a week. Gretchen had a spunky voice; I just knew I'd like her. We made plans a few weeks later for Gretchen to visit us on a Thursday for lunch. It was snowing pretty heavily that day where Gretchen lived, so she called me to see how it was up our way. I told her it looked clear. Gretchen was supposed to be over by noon. When she didn't make it by 1:30, I knew something was wrong. She called to say she'd been in an accident with a county snowplow. The family car was a mess but she was okay. I think we're both glad she at least tried to make it that day. . . . Two days later, Elizabeth died.

Calling Gretchen to tell her Elizabeth had died was the hardest phone call I've ever had to make. We talked a few times over the next two days. We discovered we were experiencing a lot of the same feelings. We both felt bad that family and friends were hurting for us. We wished we didn't have to put everyone through this. But really, how can you tell people who love you not to hurt when they know you're feeling more pain that you ever believed possible.

The first time we saw Gretchen was at the funeral home. We recognized her right away. Her face was Elizabeth's. I'll never forget standing in front of Elizabeth's casket, side by side with Gretchen, our arms around each other. To me, this was open adoption at its most comforting, most sharing level. It's been almost two years since Elizabeth died. When I write or speak to Gretchen of Elizabeth, I know her feelings. . . . They are my own.

Gabriel

A couple of months after Elizabeth died, we moved back to the Traverse City area. We were only in our new house two weeks when I got a call from Jim. (He must have gotten our number from information; I hadn't given it to him yet.) He said he had a three-month-old boy named Gabriel that he wanted to tell me about. Gabriel didn't have any medical problems, but because he was bi-racial (his father was black) he was in something of a special category—the kind of category that apparently brings the Rybickis to mind for some people.

I called Rick at work and told him about Gabe. Rick had been hoping for another girl. He kept saying, "Are you sure Jim didn't say it's a bi-racial *girl*?" Anyway, I called Jim back and we made arrangements to pick up Gabe at the Popp's house that evening. (We figure if there is a next time, we'll just bypass the agency and go right to the Popp's house!) We could tell by the way Mr. Popp was holding Gabe that he was very special to them. They were surprised to see how grown-up Rachel had gotten. Rachel thought it was great to get a brother and wanted to take him home right away.

We met Gabe's birthmom, Pam, at the agency the next day. We talked quite a bit about her family and got a little information on Gabe's birthfather. Pam could see that Rachel was crazy about her brother-to-be, and I knew this reassured her that Gabe would be happy with us. When we saw Pam again a few months later, we mentioned that Gabe should be part Italian, the way he loves spaghetti. Pam said, "He *is* part Italian, didn't I tell you? I'm part Italian myself." That's one of the best things about open adoption—if you have a question about your child, you've always got someone to ask, and if you've got a "cute moment" to share, there's always someone who thinks it's as wonderful as you do.

Kristi

Around Thanksgiving of 1985, Abbie from CFCS called and asked if we'd be interested in having a young lady who was pregnant live with us until she delivered her baby. Thinking she was speaking theoretically, I said, "Sure."

"Great," she said, "her name is Kristi and she needs a place to stay in a week or so."

As it turned out, Kris stayed with another family until January, then came to stay with us. We'd never had anyone live with us before, so we didn't really know what to expect. As it turned out, things went pretty well. It did feel a little strange, though, to go shopping with a young pregnant girl and know that everyone thinks she's your daughter. There were times when I felt like Kris' mom, which was weird because she was going to be a mom soon. Most of all, though, we became friends. She shared her life and feelings with me, and I shared mine with her. Rachel was sometimes in awe of Kris (after all, Kris was a *teenager*), and other times, they verbally sparred—a lot like sisters. Gabe enjoyed having a second mom around. And Rick pretty cheerfully made a few adjustments (like not walking around in his underwear).

In March, Kris chose an adoptive couple for her baby. She seemed so happy and relieved when she came home from her first meeting with them. We had them over for dinner; after all, we felt like we had a small stake in this baby, too. We "approved", so things were allowed to proceed.

I went with Kris to some of her doctor appointments, social service meetings, and, finally, to the childbirth class. I gained a new respect for my children's birthmoms. I could see up close the physical and emotional changes they must have gone through. I could now almost imagine how it must have felt to carry a child for nine months and then turn this baby over to be raised and loved by someone else. I know Kris was reassured by the open and caring relationship she had already established with Nancy and Dave (the adoptive parents). I felt better after meeting them, also.

Kris delivered Sara three days before her scheduled C-Section. Nancy and Dave were there at the hospital. I shared in their joy while I watched them bathe Sara for the first time. I shared Kris' grief when she came home from the hospital to our house empty-handed. I think this is what open adoption is about, too—coming to terms with another's pain in the midst of your own joy.

As a final note, we feel we have been so lucky to have had the love and support of our families through all of our open adoption experiences. Our children truly have the best of both worlds; they know they are totally accepted and loved by our families, and they are still a part of their birthparents' families. After all, children can never have too much love.

Brenda and Mike Swander

"I felt the pain and exhaustion"

It was only a five-hour drive, but it seemed like an eternity. We reckoned that we had never had a meeting quite like the one we were rolling toward and we weren't really sure what it would be like.

The call had come two weeks earlier, on March 5th. A woman identifying herself as Paula phoned and mentioned that the agency had been working with her. She went on to share the stunning news that she had picked Mike and me to be the adoptive parents of her child. Paula explained that when she looked through all the albums of potential adoptive parents, she kept coming back to ours. She also said that her mother had independently reached the same conclusion. I could feel within myself a growing sense that this was meant to be—that it was real.

As the conversation proceeded, I learned that Paula was 23, single, and already had a three-year-old son which her parents were helping to raise. She felt that she could not handle the financial or emotional strains of raising another child. She told us that the birthfather was unhelpful even to the point of denying paternity. Paula had seen her son raised without benefit of a father and wanted this child to have a father's love.

The phone call was most cordial. Somewhere along the way Paula put her mother, Donna, on the line and she sounded just as pleasant as Paula. By the time our chat wound down, we were all eager to get together and we made arrangements for the earliest possible opportunity.

By the time our five-hour eternity ended and we pulled up in front of Paula's house, our eagerness had mostly faded into fear. We rallied whatever calmness we could muster, issued our silent prayers, and knocked on the door.

We were welcomed with the sort of warmth usually reserved for missing family members. We met Paula's complete family, something most adoptive families probably don't get to do—her parents, John and Donna; her son, Tim; her brother, John; and her sisters Betsy, Diane, and Stella.

We talked about the adoption and Paula's situation and a little bit of everything, and found that we all really had a lot of the same interests. Paula told us that her due date was April 25th and we were elated to think that in just two and one-half months we would be parents. We had planned on visiting for only three hours or so, but ended up staying most of the day and even for supper. We felt completely comfortable and didn't want to leave. We knew that we had found not only our child to adopt, but some really good friends in the Adamses. They are a very warm and loving family. We found our ideas and wants as far as the rearing of the child to be the same as Paula's. From the very first moment, we all felt that God really had a hand in the arrangement.

Paula told us everything about her doctor's visit and how the baby was doing. She even gave us some ultrasound pictures of the baby, which I was every excited to have. I felt so much a part of her pregnancy, and our bond as mothers had begun. Paula stressed that she would like for me to be in the delivery room with her and this was one thing that I really wanted to do. I was so excited to be able to be such a big part of our child's delivery. It seemed like everything we wanted they wanted, and vice versa. It was great!

After the first visit, we talked several times in the phone and it was a couple of weeks before we were able to get back down to see them. Again we were greeted like part of the family. Paula even invited me to go to some of her doctor's visits with her so we decided to stay an extra day. We started going down to their house every weekend so that I could go to the doctor with Paula.

She had already explained to the doctors and nurses about the adoption and they were very supportive and helpful.

Mike and I were contacted by the head nurse of the maternity ward at the University of Michigan Hospital and she invited us to come by so she could show us around. We met there and she gave us the grand tour. They all seemed happy and excited to be part of this adoption, and we really appreciated their friendliness.

I was able to be right with Paula through her medical examinations. The doctor said that the baby was doing well and that Paula's due date was moved up to April 11th. This doubled our excitement. On March 21st, I heard the heartbeat of the child Mike and I were to adopt. Words could never express the joy I felt. Paula made me very much a part of her pregnancy; she let Mike and me both feel the baby move and told us everything about how she was feeling and what the baby was doing.

On April 3rd, Donna called and Paula was having some serious labor pains and was going to the hospital. Immediately, Mike and I took off for Ann Arbor. We didn't really talk much on the way; both our minds were going 100 miles an hour and it took an effort to make sure the car didn't do the same. We just wanted to be there! We met Paula in the labor room. She was having pains but they were very erratic; soon after we arrived, they quit completely.

Over the next two weeks, we experienced three more trips of false labor, all exciting and nervous. We continued to go down on weekends and I continued to go with Paula to the doctor. They kept saying that she was going to having this baby "just any day." Each false labor, they would say, "Yes, Paula, this is real," but the pains would quit as quickly as they came. Paula made the comment that this was probably going to be a very stubborn child! Ha! With each visit, we grew closer and closer to Paula and her family and her baby. Our bond just kept growing and growing.

On April 15th, we decided to go downstate to Kalamazoo where we would only be one hour from Paula instead of five, to await the arrival of this stubborn child. On April 18th, we experienced the fifth false labor. This time they kept Paula a long time and we had to walk her in the halls to bring on the labor more forcibly. They really felt she was ready; she just wasn't dilating. So we walked the halls of the hospital for two hours but this child just wasn't ready.

When they released Paula to go home, they instructed us to walk her legs off the next day, so walk we did. We took her to the mall and walked and walked and walked, but to no avail, right then! Paula was so good-natured about the whole thing but she began to really tire and wanted this baby to come. She even tried an old wives' remedy, using castor oil to bring on labor; all this did for her was to make her walk more and more, to and from the restroom.

On April 29th, at 12:30 A.M., we received a call from Donna that, once again, Paula was in serious labor and was leaving for the hospital. So off we headed for Ann Arbor. By this time, we knew our routine at the hospital, and the nurses and doctors didn't questions who we were and what we were doing; they just wished us good luck! When I arrived at the labor room, Paula was having contractions 45 seconds apart and lasting 60 to 70 seconds. Everyone, including the doctors, was sure that this was it, but at 5:00 A.M., this child decided not to join us yet and they sent Paula home, expecting her back within 24 hours. We were all exhausted and began to wonder if Paula was really pregnant or not.

The next day (the morning of the 30th), I called my mother in Indiana to give her a progress report, and she laughed and told me that it would not be until the next day because there was a full moon on the 31st and the baby would be sure to come the next morning. I sure hoped she was right! I told her that the labor was really killing me. It's funny how, throughout Paula's many trips of false labor, though I know my pains were not as strong as hers, I felt the pain and exhaustion of her labor.

On May 1st at 5:00 A.M., Donna called and Paula was once again on her way to the hospital. She had been timing her pains for four hours and they were even stronger than ever before. Maybe my mom was going to be right! Off we went to Ann Arbor again. Something was different. Mike and I both knew that this was it; we just questioned whether we would make it to the delivery or not.

We arrived at the hospital at 7:08 and I went on up to the labor floor while Mike parked the car. Upon entering the maternity area, I approached the nurse's desk and asked which room Paula was in or had she been sent home again? They all looked at each other and one of the nurses asked whether I wanted to see Paula or my baby. My heart stopped! I walked into Paula's room and there she lay, looking exhausted, and there sat her sister Betsy with her eyes full of tears and the first thing I said was "Did I miss it?" Paula began to cry and said, "You have a girl, Mommy—an 8 lb. 11 oz., 20 inch, beautiful girl!"

I must have screamed for the nurses told me later that everyone on the third floor heard me. They, too, were caught with tears of joy in their eyes as Paula told me the news. After I finished hugging everyone in sight, Paula told me that she arrived at the hospital at 5:26 A.M. and was dilated to 9. The baby came 22 minutes later. She had been so stubborn before, but when she decided to come, she came! Betsy began telling me all about being in there with Paula and how wonderful it was. I really felt as if I were there, too! She kept saying how beautiful the baby was and how healthy. My disappointment at not being there soon disappeared because Paula's having Betsy there with her was a really special thing for these sisters.

Paula looked at me and said, "Go get Daddy and go see your little girl." So Betsy took me out to find Mike. He was just getting out of the elevator and when he saw me, he knew he was a Daddy. When I told him we had a girl, he grabbed me and hugged me and the tears fell again and he said, "Let's go see our girl."

Betsy took us to the nursery and the nurse was expecting us. There were about six or eight babies in there. Over on the far side of the room was this beautiful pink naked girl lying under a lamp and we knew she was ours. The nurse laughed and said, "Yep, she's yours." We walked over to her and we were both crying. She was so beautiful; lots of hair and so little. I first checked to make sure she had ten fingers and ten toes, and they were all there! They had not completely cleaned her up from birth because they wanted us to give her her first bath.

The nurse wrapped her in a blanket and handed her to her daddy and I will never forget the look on his face—his eyes were fulls of tears and he looked scared to death. He handled her like she was going to break right in half. The nurse laughed and said,

"She won't break, Daddy." We then gave her her bath and took turns feeding her. Our bond with Jennifer Lynn had begun. She ate real well and soon fell asleep. There is nothing in the world sweeter than having your baby fall asleep in your arms.

The nurses gave us some classes on infant care that really helped us, then told us that the pediatrician would be in later to check her all over and that if she continued to do as well as she was, we would probably take her home that very day.

While Jennifer Lynn slept, we returned to Paula's room where she, too, was resting. We all cried and hugged and hugged and cried and talked about how beautiful Jennifer was. Mike and I found it very hard to find the words to tell Paula how very happy she had made us. The bond that we felt with her was even stronger and richer than before.

While the doctor was in checking Paula, we were downstairs at the pay phones calling everyone! The joy and excitement we could feel while telling our families and friends was wonderful. They had all been so supportive and excited throughout the whole adoption procedure. Later, when we talked to Paula, she said that she wanted us to bring Jennifer into her room as much as we could and the four of us to all be together. So most of the day was spent in her room. We had a wonderful time and this will, for sure, be a day to tell Jennifer about when she is older. Paula was so very strong and loving.

After the pediatrician had checked Jennifer and told us that everything with her was going great and that she was a perfectly healthy baby, he told us that we could take her home. We were so excited and nervous because we knew that this was going to be hard for Paula. When we returned to Paula's room, we found that the nurse had told her we were taking Jennifer home that night. She was lying in her bed and crying hard. It was such an emotional time; we really didn't know what to say to her and she didn't know what to say to us. We tried to reassure her that this was not goodbye forever and that we would be seeing each other again and that she could call us any time. She did say, "Please tell Jennifer someday that this is the hardest thing I have ever had to do and that I love her very much!" We reassured her that Jennifer would know this and that she would know what a wonderful and loving birthmother she has.

Paula was having such a rough time we felt really guilty about taking Jennifer but she kept telling us that this is truly what she wanted and we knew, also, that it was the right decision for Paula in her circumstances. One of her friends was there and she told us that Paula just wanted us to go . . . that she was having a hard time mainly because we were leaving with Jennifer and she was going to have to stay up in the maternity ward with all the other mothers and babies. Later we found out that Paula's mother, Donna, convinced the doctor to let Paula leave that night also.

It was a strange trip back to Kalamazoo. We were happy and excited but also sad for Paula. We also felt nervousness because we knew that Paula could change her mind if she wanted to, but deep in our hearts, we knew that she wouldn't do this because she knew that what she was doing was the right thing.

Our first night with our daughter was probably like all parents' first night with a newborn. She slept more than we did! We lay awake watching her every breath. It was wonderful! Early the next morning Donna called to tell us that Paula really felt bad about how she was when we left and that she wanted to reassure us that everything was okay. She did ask us to come by and see them on Sunday on our way home. We told her that we would but we were afraid that when we had to leave it would be really hard on Paula again.

When we got to their house, it was a whole different story. Paula wanted to let us know again how sure she was that she had made the right decision. She just wanted to see the three of us together. She did tell us that we probably would not see a lot of her for awhile because she really wanted to try and get her life back together and to work on her relationship with her son, Timmy. They had told Timmy that the baby Mommy was carrying was for Mike and Brenda, and that is how he really wanted it to be. When we left, we felt a lot better about how Paula was feeling.

We arrived home early Sunday afternoon and showed Jennifer her new home. It was another day we will never forget.

The weeks seemed to fly by. Jennifer was growing so fast. Mike and I truly believed we were the happiest couple on earth. On June 25th, Paula went to court to sign off all her legal rights to Jennifer. After leaving court, she and her parents came by for a short visit. Paula was having no second thoughts about her decision. It was good to see them and we knew that we would be seeing them again.

Paula's mother and I called each other about every other week and we wrote and sent pictures back and forth. She told us that Paula was energetically trying to get her life back together and was still unsure about how much we would see her right away. We understood that she would need time, but were also sure that she would call us soon.

Early in October, Paula called and said that she had three days off and wondered if she could come for a visit. We really looked forward to seeing her but I have to admit that I was nervous. I've been told such apprehension was perfectly normal. She arrived on Monday afternoon and couldn't get over how much Jennifer had grown. We had a pretty good visit. It was a little emotional and tense, but I guess that is normal, too. I couldn't help but feel a little jealous and scared. It made us all realize how careful we would have to be with Jennifer to make sure she is not confused by the arrangement. Paula does not want Jennifer told about adoption until she is quite a bit older because she is afraid that Jennifer will hate her. We believe that Jennifer should be told gradually as her capacity for understanding grows. We are confident she will mirror our feeling and will accept Paula and her family as the wonderful people they are.

When I think back to the whole birth experience, I wouldn't have had anything any different—not even the six false labors—because it all seemed to happen just like it was supposed to. I do wish that we had planned ahead better about the hospital departure; it perhaps would have been easier on all of us.

We feel strongly about open adoption. The opportunity to be part of the birth experience is priceless. We will have so much to tell Jennifer about the whole incredible experience. Our enthusiasm is bound to help her understand that she was a treasured child from the very beginning and that her birthmother truly did what she felt was best for her.

Because of Paula, we have received the child we have always wanted. We have also added wonderful friends into our lives, not only with the Adams family, but also with the adoption agency. They helped us prepare for everything and are wonderful people to know and count as friends.

Don and Kathy Spinniken

"Truly, gifts from God"

She caught the bouquet and I caught the garter. Although that sounds like a fairy tale, it's true; that is how it all started with Kathy and me. It was at the wedding of her friend the bride and my friend the groom and although we laughed at it at the time, in hindsight, maybe the bouquet and garter thing was a little part of destiny. As you will see, many aspects of this story read like a wonderful fairy tale, like a "made in heaven" story, and that's exactly the point I'm trying to make.

First of all, my wife and I decided to be friends, best friends, then we decided to get married. We made a commitment to be best friends for a million years or forever, whichever comes later. We're sure that this friendship as a base to our relationship will give us the staying power we desire.

After being married for about a year, Kathy and I decided to start a family, to share our love with children. "Decided to start" might not be the right phrase here; we did start to Try. After a short time of no success, we started checking with the doctors and clinics to find out why. Without going into detail let me say that we did learn enough about human reproduction to be amazed that anybody *ever* gets pregnant at all! Back to our case, let's just say that without a definitive cause and, of course, no known "cure" for our infertility, we did not and have not become "natural" parents—through no lack of effort on our part!

While in the process of studying our infertility we talked with many of our friends and acquaintances and learned of several happy experiences with adoption that some of these friends had had. We decided to explore adoption concurrently with our infertility work-ups and so made our first contact with Community, Family and Children Services. At our first meeting our caseworker told us that the agency did adoptions a little differently from many others and gave us a very brief overview of "openness" in adoption. He told us that if we weren't interested in exploring new ideas that perhaps we should check other agencies. He also told us that if we *were* interested, we'd learn more during a series of educational meetings and that if we decided later that the program wasn't for us, we could bow out gracefully.

We were a little skeptical at first, but thought, "What the heck, let's check it out!" The meetings were very educational indeed. We attended several group meetings with about ten other "prospective adoptive parents" couples. The best way for me to describe it was that I learned to "wear the other person's moccasins" in the sense that I tried to put myself in the position of the adoptee and think and feel like he/she would through the whole adoption experience and through life; to put myself in the position of a birthparent and think and feel how she would think and feel through, and especially *after*, the adoption experience.

Each couple then sat down privately with a caseworker, going over more personal things like family history, health, heritage, beliefs, financial stability, etc. Next came a meeting with about five prospective adoptive couples and five or six birthmoms. (Yes, in the same room!) The birthmoms ranged from teen to middle age, having released their offspring to adoption anywhere from twenty years ago to a few months before our meeting. There was even one who was pregnant and working with the agency, contemplating adoption as an option for her yet unborn child. Her name was Lynette.

I was nervous. I also was saddened to hear some of the stories these women told about not being allowed to see their babies after they were born, not knowing to this day if their child was all right or even alive. Then I got mad. It made me mad to think that some entity, some law could do this to these women "for their own good." I'm a man so I'll never bear a child and yet I know that I could never carry a child for nine months, give birth, and then *forget* it ever happened. I couldn't convince myself of such a lie and I can't ask any birthparents to try and tell such a lie to themselves. As a parent now of two adopted children, I can't and won't perpetrate that kind of deception on them; it's no basis for the kind of relationship I want with my children.

Back to the story. We are now a part of a group of five couples and we now attend a meeting in each of our homes with the caseworker in attendance to see our homes and finish the educational phase of our preparation for becoming adoptive parents. It was at one of these meetings that I told Jim, our caseworker, that I was so convinced of the rightness of openness in adoption that, as much as Kathy and I wanted a child, I didn't feel I could ever accept a closed adoption arrangement. I felt that strongly about it.

We're not sure why, we just felt that we were somewhere near being chosen (give or take six months), but anyway Kathy gave the company she worked for two weeks notice. The next thing you know, Jim calls and asks if we'd be able to come into his office the next day because Lynette—yes, the birthmom we'd met at the meeting—wanted to ask us a few more questions! Yes, of course we could come!

Lynette asked me how I was. I said I was nervous. She said she was too and so we stood there in the middle of the room for a minute until finally she said, "Let's sit down." After Lynette had asked us a few questions, really just clarifications on answers we had submitted to agency questionnaires earlier, Kathy told Lynette that it seemed a little unfair in that there was only one of her and we didn't know how many other couples she might be considering. It was then that she told us that she had all but decided to place her child for adoption and that we were the people she wanted to be her child's parents. Huge sigh!

Lynette was very glad to see how happy we were with that news and that's why she kept it secret, because she wanted to share that moment with us. You see, we were the first people who were happy about and rejoiced in the life that was growing inside her.

From that moment on we have been the best of friends. It's like we adopted Lynette at the same time we adopted our son, Matthew. She is like an extended family member; we love her totally, unconditionally, and forever, and she loves us. I am humbled by the fact that this woman *chose* to love us enough that she would entrust the upbringing of her child to us. We "owe" her a lot and the only "pay" she'll accept is the love that Matthew, Kathy, (and now Amy), and I freely give to her.

Lynette "chose" us as prospective parents about November 11th; her due date was November 26th. When we left home early Sunday morning, November 20th, to go shopping for furniture for the nursery, Lynette still had a week to go before her due date. When we got home with the changing-table that evening and retrieved from the answering machine several "beeps" with no messages attached, we jokingly said that Lynette must have gone into labor but didn't want to say such a thing on "that damned machine."

Within minutes, Rick, Lynette's friend and birth "coach", called to say they'd been trying all afternoon to reach us but didn't want to talk to the answering machine. It seems that Lynette *was* in labor; however, it was progressing very slowly and so Rick said to stay home, get some sleep, and he'd call in the morning. Get some sleep? Ha! Early the next morning Rick called and told us they were going to try and induce delivery of the baby and that we should come to the hospital to "man" the maternity waiting room. "Waiting" room is an understatement. We arrived at about 10 o'clock in the morning and we waited . . . and waited . . . and waited. Every two or three hours Rick would come out of the L.D.R. (labor-delivery-recovery) room to report to us on Lynette's progress . . . slow.

Early in the day there were several other people in the waiting room with us, waiting for a wife, daughter, sister to have a baby. One by one the nurses came and our fellow waiters left to see the new arrivals until finally, late in the afternoon, we were the only ones left in the room. The double doors to the delivery area were almost directly across the hall from the waiting room and so when the nurses came out of those doors carrying a little "bundle" we were on the edges of our seats. Then one of the nurses looked right at us and scolded, 'Well, come on!" We jumped and ran to follow!

The nurses were great! They knew we were the prospective adoptive parents of this baby and insisted that we scrub our hands, put on gowns, and see and touch this baby immediately! They even kept the baby covered until the last minute and would not tell us the baby's gender before we got in the nursery to be with . . . him! It's a boy! I can't believe it! We're holding his hand and talking to him and he's only ten minutes old! It's a miracle, it really is! We even call him Matthew because Kathy and I had picked names, boy and girl, before we had even met Lynette. Lynette had told us when she was at our house for dinner the previous Friday that she thought the names we had chosen for our baby were fine and she even wrote them down so that she'd spell it right.

So Matthew's name has been Matthew from the day he was born. However, Matthew's middle name was adjusted slightly. Kathy and I made up a boy's name by combining a couple of our great-grandfather's names, Matthew and Heinrich. After a long labor and delivery a very tired Lynette wrote on the hospital birth certificate: Matthew Hein*rick* with a "k" and we *all* agreed that in honor of Lynette's friend, "Uncle" Rick, who was there for Lynette through all of that long labor and delivery, we should leave the spelling with the "k."

After seeing and talking to Matthew for about an hour, the nurses took him back to Lynette in the L.D.R. room. We felt that they should be alone for a while so we left the hospital to get something to eat. It was, after all, about 7:30 in the evening and we hadn't eaten since breakfast, being afraid to leave that waiting room all day!

When we returned to see if Lynette was in her room yet, Rick came out from the L.D.R. room and said "Get in here, we've been looking for you", so we put on hospital gowns and went in. As we came in Lynette looked up at us and said "We have a son!" Then she held Matthew up to me and asked, "Would you like to hold your son!" You know the answer!

That was all on Monday and we brought Matthew home from the hospital on Thursday, Thanksgiving Day 1983, *three days old!* Indeed, we had much to give thanks for on that day and every day since then. We continue to have an open and loving relationship with Lynette.

(Without offending any nursing mothers I want to inject here that one advantage of bottle-fed babies is that, if dad participates as I did, with each of us trading every other night of getting up to meet the baby's needs, dad also gets to bond and spend precious time with his newborn baby.)

And Then Came Amy

Not flesh of my flesh, nor bone of my bone
But still miraculously my own
Never forget for a single moment
You didn't grow under my heart,
But in it.

This is the way I feel about my two adopted children. They are miracles. God has entrusted their care to Don and me. He did this by way of very special birthparents. Don has described the story of our first child, Matthew. Matthew is now four years old and our relationship with Lynette continues to grow stronger. She is a part of our family. We still raise a few eyebrows and are asked a lot of questions by people who have always thought of adoption as a closed process, but our relationship with Lynette is very natural and easy.

About two years ago Don and I decided we were ready for another child. Matthew said he wanted a Baby to put in the crib since he was a Big Boy and slept in the Big Bed now. So we stopped by the agency one day and Matthew told our caseworker that he wanted to be a Big Brother. The caseworker took Matthew by the hand and said "Let's talk about this in my office." Of course we were asked to come along also.

We had to update our paperwork and also attend a few meetings with one other second-time adoptive couple and about ten first-time prospective adoptive parents. The whole process was not anywhere near as involved the second time around as the first. We were, however, a little anxious, and as with any prospective parent the wait seemed forever.

After about eight months of waiting, we decided we needed

to get away from the stress of the everyday rat race, so we headed south to Georgia where my brother, Bill, and his family live. We had a whole week of fun planned, and my folks from Tennessee were coming down to join us the end of the week. Well, things always happen when you least expect them. We had arrived at my brother's on Sunday night. Monday afternoon we got a call from Michigan telling us that a little girl was born that morning and wanted to meet us! We met Amy's birthmom, Lisa, for the first time by telephone, long distance. By the second call we were like old friends. Amy's birthparents are younger than Matthew's and the driving distance between us is greater than with Lynette, but we have a very special bond with them.

As it turned out we were not able to return home before Amy was released from the hospital. We own a small airplane and that is how we had traveled to Georgia. Since the weather would not cooperate with us, we were not able to leave the south until Thursday morning and that was the day Amy and Lisa were released from a downstate hospital. Of course by this time all of our families and our friends had been informed about our new daughter. Someone had to make the trip downstate for us, to pick up Amy, so we called Don's mom and dad who live about 300 yards or so from our house. We asked them if they would be able to drive downstate to pick up their newest grandchild. To say the least they were honored. In fact Granddad remarked later that it was a lot more fun being a participant that to sit home making his own meals while Grandma got to go help with the new babies.

Lisa seemed thrilled that she would get a chance to meet Amy's grandparents also. Little did she know that that would *not* be the last time they would meet. We arrived home about an hour before Don's parents arrived with Amy. Amy was so-o-o-o tiny! She weighed 5 lb. 12 oz. and 18¼ inches long, such a difference from Matthew's 8 lb. 2 oz. and 21½ inches. Matthew immediately wanted to help, he was so proud to be a Big Brother!

We continued over the next week to talk with Lisa by phone. We were anxious to meet each other and wanted to put faces with voices. The weekend before Amy turned two weeks old we drove downstate to meet Amy's birthparents. We spent the afternoon at

Lisa's house and met all of her immediate family. We also met Amy's birthfather and *his* mom. We were a little nervous at first, but within minutes we were all very comfortable and enjoying a Sunday afternoon visiting with family.

Two days later Lisa and her mom drove to Northern Michigan for a court date so that Lisa, age 16 at that time, could relinquish her maternal rights to Amy. The hearing was not until 4 o'clock in the afternoon, after which they came out to our house for dinner and spent the night. In fact, Lisa's mom insisted that *they* would get up with Amy that night. They said it would be a pleasure for them. Of course, we thought a full night's sleep would be pleasurable also!

I would never begin to say that giving up their children for adoption was an easy decision for either Lynette or Lisa, but they constantly tell us how much easier we make it for them because they see their children happy, healthy, and extremely loved. By having all the unknowns answered they feel much better about their decision.

Lisa has made the trip up north two more times. Each trip she stays with us and gets a lot of hands-on experience with Amy.

We hope that our children will grow up with good feelings about their heritage. We hope that we can always be truthful with them and be able to answer all their questions about their birthparents. If we don't have an answer they can go straight to the source. There are no fixed rules or visitations; also, if you ask either set of birthparents they will tell you that Don and Kathy are Amy's and Matthew's "Real Parents."

Children truly are gifts from God and in our case so are birthparents. We know He has had His hand in the putting together of our family which now includes Kathy, Don, Matthew, and Amy. Our family also includes Lynette, Matthew's birthmom, and Amy's birthparents, Terry and Lisa, who said they chose us because after hearing and reading about our relationship with Lynette they wanted the same kind of relationship with us.

This is where the fairy tale usually says "and they lived happily ever after." Well, we can't be sure about that but we do know that the future promises a lot of shared *love* between some very special people. We thank God often for bringing us all together.

Kathy and Mark Olson

"A lot of hurting, crying, and waiting"

After one successful birth (Davey in 1981), we tried having more children but I miscarried twice in the third and fifth months. We had always wanted a big family so we sought medical help. After exploratory surgery on March 4, 1984, doctors planned to use fertility drugs to encourage a pregnancy. They had us convinced that we'd have sextuplets and (surprisingly to most people) we were ecstatic about that! However, two days after surgery, doctors found that I had uterine cancer. We were devastated. They had to perform a complete hysterectomy. Mark and I were 26 years old and Davey three at the time, so it was a tremendous setback for us. Fortunately, our faith in God is so strong that nothing can keep us down for long!

At the time, we were so grateful that I would survive that nothing else mattered. But about two weeks after surgery, we realized our dream of having a large family was no longer possible. Davey is such a bubbly, happy boy that it is no wonder we wanted about seven more just like him! Both Mark and I had grown up in large families: five boys on his side and eight girls and one boy on my side. We saw how much fun and love there was in large families and, more than ever, we wanted this kind of life for Davey.

It's funny, but during the five years we dated, we talked about adoption often, in case we were never able to bear our own children. We feel that God must have been showing us, even then, what our next decision would be. And to make sure we followed that plan, we found Community, Family and Children Services without searching, as well! Mark, in his travels out and about the community, encountered a lady holding a beautiful baby boy. They started talking and the woman told Mark she worked for CFCS and the baby was going to his new home that day. Mark came home so excited that the following morning we called the agency. One week later we attended the first information meeting. We were excited about the "openness" but skeptical. We thought that we would always have to worry about our child being stolen by his birthparents, or the child wanting to go live with them. But as you will see later in our story, it's exactly that fear that "open adoption" eliminates.

We officially applied in May, 1984, and because of the cancer I had had, the agency held our file for one year. They wanted assurance that the cancer was truly gone. That first year of waiting wasn't easy but we can understand their concern. In May, 1985, our home study began. "Home study" sounds tame but it really bares your soul. For us it was almost like a marriage encounter course; at the same time, it revealed to the agency exactly the kind of people we are and the kind of parents we would be. It also made us really think about our values and our opinions on family issues.

Throughout those two months of study our friends were all supportive but really couldn't imagine what we were going through. Davey was growing older by the minute and we wanted him to have a brother or sister so badly. He was then five and going to day care/preschool and I constantly heard from other parents and the teacher how Davey was so good with *their* children. One mother called to thank me because Davey taught her children to hug! All of this just kept us going as we waited for our child.

In January, 1986, we were entered into a support group of five couples. This group was an outlet for our frustrations and fears, and a bond developed that exists still. We continue to meet once a month and feel that we will keep this up to help us deal with anything that emerges as our children go through various life phases.

Then in May, 1986 (two days after Mother's Day), the call came!

Jim phoned our office and told me that we had "been chosen"! I said, "Oh, my gosh!" and quickly sat down—before I fell down. Jim started to tell me some of the background about Darla (our birthmom) but my head was whirling so fast I had to ask him if I could put him on hold while I ran to get my husband. My knees and hands were shaking and I was close to hyperventilating. Mark was just coming around the corner to tell me the accountant was on hold on the phone for over ten minutes and why hadn't I spoken to him. I beamed from ear to ear and said, "Because I'm talking to the adoption agency and we have been chosen!" His face went white and he said, "You're kidding!" Even though we applied with the idea of receiving a baby, it doesn't seem real until you get that call!

We met with Jim later that same day. He had pictures of Darla and of her first child as a baby and instantly tears came into our eyes. We were given Darla's background and told that she was due on June 25th. We had six weeks to wait. We were told that we could call her and set up a meeting or have the adoption agency do so.

We left the agency and hurried to pick up Davey (now 5½) from day care. We told him that we had a surprise for him and asked him what he wanted most in the world. He said, "A baby!" and gave us the biggest hug. That night, we sat down and wrote a letter to Darla thanking her for choosing us, and we mailed it that night.

Two days later, there was a message on our answering machine from Darla saying that she'd like to meet us. Mark wanted me to call her immediately (easy for him to say) but I needed a few moments to gather my composure. After thinking it over and praying for the words to be there, I took a deep breath and called Darla. Somehow the words flowed and we set up a time to meet one week from that day.

All week we were nervously awaiting the meeting. The last day, we could hardly eat or sleep, wondering if she'd like us, what to wear, would there be enough to talk about, etc. (Silly things when we think about them now.)

Finally the day came. We gave each other a hug and with butterflies in our stomach, went to her door. Darla let us in and we immediately started talking to her cute two-year-old girl, and that broke the ice. Darla said that I looked like her cousin and, from that moment on, it seemed like we had known each other for years! We talked about the baby and what we all wanted as far as openness. It seemed so easy to talk to her. It occurred to us that our friends and relatives would never believe we were sitting there talking to this woman who was going to give up her child for us! Certainly we never believed we could be that open. Before leaving, Darla asked us to feel her stomach, and the baby kicked. Then she gave us the biggest hugs and we departed with happy, yet sad feelings. We wanted a baby so much but could we hurt her like that?

We continued to meet Darla every week for nine weeks. As her due date drew nearer, she expressed her sadness more frequently. We were conscious of our fear that she might change her mind, but that wasn't as much a concern as our helping Darla get through this. We wished we could somehow shoulder the anguish for her, but all we could do was be her friends and share our excitement. Darla's due date came and went and each night we jumped if the phone rang after 11:00 P.M. Darla had no car or phone, so we knew when she did get to a phone, she would be well into labor and we would be her transportation to the hospital (a 45-minute trip from our home to hers).

Finally, three weeks overdue, Darla started labor on the way to the hospital for a stress test. However, after being admitted for two hours, doctors decided it wasn't true labor and had us take her back home! The next morning at 9:00 A.M., Darla called and said that her doctor was going to induce her as her labor kept starting and stopping. We were told to get her to the hospital at 5:00 P.M. We hung up the phone and screamed with excitement. My sisters were up for vacation and decided to stay and watch Davey while we took Darla to the hospital. (I knew they couldn't miss out on the excitement.)

Darla was really frightened and nervous, partly because she was worried that something was wrong and partly because this was *it* . . . and it was so real! We just kept her laughing and talking about how to breathe.

Upon arriving at the hospital, Darla was admitted and Jack, her fiancé (not the father), entered the labor room with her. Darla had wanted him to be her labor coach even though she wasn't confident he knew what to do. Ten minutes after she was admitted, Jack came into the waiting room and said that Darla wanted to speak to me. He wouldn't tell me why and his face gave no hint as to what was happening. Mark and I both felt that fear rise inside that she was changing her mind but our faith told us, whatever the outcome, God would help us through.

When I entered Darla's room, she was crying hysterically. I asked her what was the matter and we held hands as she tried to talk. She finally told me she had been crying because she wanted a private room afterward instead of sharing a room with a new mom who would be keeping her baby. We solved the problem, and after calming her down I left the labor room heaving another sigh of relief.

Then the waiting began. . . . How awful it must be for fathers who sit in the waiting room until their child is born instead of being in the labor/delivery rooms with their wives. Talk about pacing! Two couples from our adoption group came up to offer support and we found their thoughtfulness very sustaining. After 30 minutes, Jack came out for a break and I offered to go into the labor room and help Darla until he felt ready to return. I held her hand and helped her to breathe. Jack returned but after two hours he couldn't stomach seeing Darla in pain and developed an affection for frequent breaks, so I remained with Darla for the remaining eight hours of labor.

As Darla's contractions became stronger, she talked more and more about why she was giving up her child and the bond between us seemed as if we were sisters. Finally, I could tell her contractions were so strong that birth was near. I paged the nurse and had barely gotten my greens on when Darla said that she had "to push." We never made it to the delivery room because five minutes later, Darla gave birth to a beautiful boy (Jayme Robert, 6 lbs. 10 oz., at 3:05 A.M.) on the labor bed. When I saw Jayme, I instantly cried and kept saying, "He's so beautiful, Darla." She didn't say anything but was concerned that I was happy he was a boy. She need not have worried . . . I was ecstatic.

The nurse asked that the father take the baby to the nursery to be cleaned up. Jack headed out but then came back and said that I had better take the baby to the nursery. I happily accepted the assignment and triumphantly marched down the hall cradling in my arms the world's most beautiful baby. Mark, who was starving for news, intercepted us. Enroute to the nursery I told him that we had a boy, a beautiful boy, and that it had been the most beautiful birth I'd ever seen.

Having turned Jayme over safely to the nursery staff, we jumped up and down like two little kids. It was wonderful . . . I had helped to bring this child into the world! We knew at that moment, in our hearts, that Darla would never change her mind because we had shared this most beautiful miracle of life together.

After one hour, I convinced the nurses to let me take Jayme to see Darla (they normally wait two hours). For some reason, we felt no fear in doing so. . . this beautiful boy had two moms and a dad who loved him very much. I handed Jayme to Darla and left them alone. After twenty minutes, Darla called us in and handed Jayme to us. A nurse came in to ask Darla if she wanted him circumcised and she said, "You'll have to ask his parents." This really startled the nurse and thrilled me.

About 7:00 A.M. we took Jack home and had just gotten home ourselves when the hospital called. Carla wanted to leave the hospital by 4:00 P.M. so we were to pick up Jayme by then. We were too excited to sleep so after showering and breaking the news to Davey, our folks, and relatives, we went right back to the hospital. *Nothing* could ever have prepared us for that moment. Darla had shown very little emotion after Jayme was born but now we could tell she had been crying, and for a long time. My sisters came into Darla's room to meet her and she talked very openly with them. They felt the specialness of Darla and the real impact that this adoption had on everyone involved. Jayme was brought in and we asked Darla if she'd like to dress him. She did while we took countless pictures.

To an outsider, it probably seemed like everyone was totally happy. But after Davey and Dad took Jayme back to the nursery, Darla couldn't contain her pain any longer. She cried so hard and

I kept rocking her in my arms and telling her how well we'd take care of him. Having had two miscarriages, I knew the emptiness she must be feeling. I kept telling her that Jayme was very lucky to have a birthmom who loved him so much that she was willing to give him up so he could have a better life than she could have given him.

The nurse came in after about an hour and helped her dress. I had gone to the waiting room to tell my sisters to wait there and knowing they knew very little about adoption, I told them exactly what was happening. They decided to wait and see us though the next couple of hours, which really added to this beautiful experience.

Davey had walked into Darla's room to say "Hi" and she was crying so he gave her a hug and came running back to me to ask why she was crying. We explained why Darla hurt so much inside and why it was so hard for her to give Jayme up. Having Davey there through those moments really showed him how special this adoption was, too.

Darla's sister arrived at about 4:00 P.M. to take her home and Darla broke down again. This time she couldn't stop crying and I asked her if she wanted to go hold Jayme and show him to her sister. The whole time she was in the nursery, we heard her crying and saw her rocking the baby. Mark and I had managed not to cry much (in front of Darla, at least), but this tore our hearts. Abbie, the CFCS social worker, came up to us and both Mark and I said we couldn't do this to Darla. We had grown to love her very much and we couldn't hurt her. I said, "I just want to give him back to her." Abbie helped us understand that both Darla and we were going through normal reactions to the situation, that we were all doing the right thing. Time would heal the hurting.

For four hours, our emotions were overflowing as we waited for Darla to prepare for leaving. We kept saying encouraging things to her, as we had for the past two months, and she smiled several times, but her sadness was so deep. Then, at 7:00 P.M., Darla was told that she could leave the hospital. After an emotional embrace, Mark and I said goodbye and nurses wheeled Darla out of the room. As soon as she left the room, we could contain ourselves no longer. We held each other and cried so hard that we felt our hearts were broken. How could the happiest day of your life be the saddest day of your life, too? My sisters cried when leaving for home, because what Darla had done for Jayme and us was so beautiful. The nurses had tears in their eyes, too. Finally, the only way I could stop crying was to go into the nursery and pick up Jayme. I rocked him and felt stronger because of this new life we had helped bring into the world. It would be all right and God would see us through these moments.

Taking Jayme home was a miracle. It seemed incredible that he was ours. We'd look at him and could only hope Darla wouldn't change her mind, because even when he was only 18 hours old we were totally in love with this beautiful child. We felt as if we had given birth to him and were just as proud as we had been when we had brought Davey home from the hospital.

On the fourth day we called Darla to see how she was feeling. We took Jayme to see her and she cried a little but said that she was definitely sure she had done the right thing. Ten days later, we took Darla to the courthouse to finalize the adoption. Normally, adoptive parents are nowhere near the courtroom when this takes place, but Darla had said that she needed our support, so we waited outside until she was through. The word "final" was the worst for her and we both gave her the biggest hugs we could and let her cry. After a while, we had her smiling again and we left to pick up Jayme and Davey. This time, she rocked Jayme in her arms for two hours and cried but you could tell she was sure about the adoption.

When we arrived at her apartment, her family had decided to surprise her and get a good look at us. This was hard at first because we saw Darla's father and grandfather (whom Jayme resembles a lot), and seeing these generations tore at our hearts as well. But after a couple of hours, we felt as if we had expanded our family further still because they were all hugging us and Darla and they said we were perfect for Jayme. As soon as they left, Darla looked at us and said, "*Now* I know I have done the right thing."

Our own court date came up about 21 days later. Darla had originally wanted to be there, but at the last moment changed her mind. (We feel this was part of her healing process.) We took pictures of the judge, the courtroom, etc. When we took the film to be developed two hours later, we discovered that the film had not been advancing in the camera and as a result there were no pictures. Being adoring parents, we had the nerve to go back to the courtroom and pull the judge out of chambers for more pictures with Jayme.

We have kept in contact with Darla by phone, letters, and one or two visits per month. Each visit shows us a more confident, happy woman and reassures us that she is totally sure of her decision. We all realize there will be times that we will fear hurt, like when Jayme at three months old looked at me and smiled but wouldn't smile for Darla. But those times will bring us all closer to Jayme and he will grow up knowing how beautiful his birthmom is. We highly respect Darla and know that she possesses more courage that anyone we know. We thank God each and every day for this miracle in our lives, and for the beautiful moments spent with Darla.

Adoption certainly is not an easy experience. There was a lot of hurting, crying, and waiting in the process of adopting Jayme, but the ultimate joy of receiving a child erases all those negative feelings. For those who are seriously considering open adoption, we have a few suggestions. We believe it is important to simply be yourselves. We believe it is extremely helpful to be part of a support group so that your fears and frustrations can be talked through. Most of all, be positive and keep the faith, *it will happen*. Although it's hard to imagine, once you hold that beautiful child, all the frustrations vanish and all that is left is a love and happiness which is beyond description.

Jane and Cam Tonn

"The goodbyes are not forever"

As I sauntered over to the retreat registration desk, I was thinking about what an odd way this was to spend our fifth wedding anniversary. We were "celebrating" the occasion by chaperoning a retreat at Concordia College in Ann Arbor for our church youth group. I turned in our names and expected a routine response. Instead, the lady at the desk became very animated and excitedly said, "We have an emergency message for you. Abbie from the adoption agency is trying to reach you. Please call her immediately." Our hearts started to race—we were stunned! We knew it must mean we had been picked.

We quickly found a phone and called Abbie in Traverse City. She told us we had indeed been picked. That wasn't the only news, either, for Abbie went on to inform us that the baby was to be born within the hour! The birthparents preferred not to meet us, but they did want us to get back to Traverse City as soon as possible to start our relationship with the baby.

What do we do now? We made several phone calls and coverage for the youth group was quickly arranged. We were free to head north. If we could have put wings on the car we would have done so. It occurred to us that we were not fully prepared to receive a baby. We hadn't started the nursery, hadn't bought a layette or decided on a name; we didn't even know if it was a boy or a girl. Well, we knew with the help of family and friends we would make short work of those details. As we travelled, we marveled at the means by which Abbie had been able to locate us. Ordinarily we do a good job of letting our families know the details when we leave town, but this time we had forgotten to do so. Getting no answer at our house, Abbie called my parents. They didn't have answers but suggested she call my brother at the family business, a fruit market. He didn't know either, but the conversation was overheard by an employee who happened to be a friend from church and who knew of our whereabouts. It seemed to us that God's hand was apparent in all this.

We arrived in Traverse City by 10:00 P.M. and went directly to the hospital. Abbie met us and explained that the birth went well. At 4 pounds 14 ounces, he (a boy!) was petite but healthy. She further explained that things had changed a little and the birthparents did want to meet us. That was fine with us since the agency's training had stimulated in us a heartfelt desire for openness. First we stole a quick peek at the baby and then went with Abbie to meet with the birthcouple. Both of them were tired from the birth experience so the meeting was fairly short. Mostly they described the ordeal of labor and delivery. We would talk more the next day.

To our surprise Abbie and the nurses set us up in a private little room with the baby. We both held and rocked him as Abbie filled us in on the baby's background. Cam and I were just as content as the baby. We were surprised to discover that the birthparents were married, but got over that feeling quickly as we realized that marriage doesn't protect people from hardship. We were told we could come everyday to see him. Basically, our privileges were just like those afforded new fathers. Our parents would also be able to visit freely. We left around midnight and I remember thinking that this wasn't such a bad anniversary after all. We had a baby. He was tiny, he was perfect, and he was ours.

The next two and a half days passed quickly. We spent ten hours a day feeding and caring for our new little baby. While he slept, we ran errands and purchased the countless necessities. Throughout our hospital stay the nurses were extraordinarily helpful. They gave us much-needed mini-lessons in bathing, diaper changing, and temperature taking.

Our baby's arrival two weeks earlier than expected changed many plans for the birthparents. They had not had time to see our photo album nor read any of our forms, and had chosen us based on Abbie's rudimentary description of us. We felt it was important for them to know us well, so we took the time to share many details of our lives with them. They were pleased that the baby had been born on our anniversary. Ann assured us that she was convinced that adoption was best for the baby since they did not feel ready for the formidable responsibilities at that point in their lives. When the time came to fill out the baby's birth certificate, they turned to us and allowed us to name him. We called him Garrett and they approved.

Ann encountered a lot of pressure from her family to change her mind, and that caused us some anxiety. We were trying to remind ourselves that it was very possible for things to change at any time prior to court; but, try as we might to "stay cool," this little bandit had stolen our hearts.

Ann wrote Garrett a beautiful letter explaining her reasons for releasing him for adoption. It was truly a letter from the heart. She wanted us to give him the letter when he would be mature enough to understand it. She wanted us to tell him that if he wanted to meet her she would be happy to do so. She felt that she would need some time to recover and that any meetings in the near future were unlikely.

Ann's mother continued to struggle with the prospect of adoption. She called us one day from the agency where she was discussing the situation with Abbie. We assured her that we would write and send pictures. We said that it would be fine with us to work out some visits. She seemed surprised that we were willing to be so open, and the prospect of ongoing communication encouraged her a great deal. She shared new background information, and by the end of our conversation it seemed that she was feeling much better about the proposed adoption. We certainly understood her need for reassurance.

Abbie called us a few times throughout the two weeks before the court date, letting us know how the birthparents were coping. We managed to stay fairly relaxed, but our own parents were very apprehensive. We were too busy with three-hour feeding intervals and countless visitors to spend any time worrying. We must admit, though, it was a welcome moment when we received the call indicating the legal release of rights had occurred.

During the first year we initiated all the communication with our birthparents and birthgrandmother. We sent six long letters detailing Garrett's accomplishments, and lots of pictures. Both families always wrote back to us immediately. We reminded them all that it might be nice to arrange a meeting. Only six months removed from the experience, Ann did not yet feel ready to meet. Her mother, on the other hand, jumped at the chance. We agreed to meet with her shortly after Garrett's birthday. We would split the 700-mile drive and meet at a motel for a day or more. As the time drew near, however, Ann indicated her discomfort with the plan and we decided to try some other time when Ann felt better about the idea.

Presently our birthparents live only a thirty-minute drive from us. As close as we live, there's lots of potential for openness, but so far they have not felt ready for it. That saddens us, but we respect their position. They know that they are welcome at any time.

A few months ago we viewed a film discussing abortion. It was hard for us to watch, for we were both struck by the dreadful thought that our smiling happy little son could easily have been the victim of such an option. We are so pleased that our birthmom was blessed with the wisdom to choose adoption. Adoption has meant new life for all of us, and we are relishing it!

Phase Two

Worn out from a weekend fishing trip, I was carefully putting away our rods and reels and conducting a mental review of all those big ones which had somehow gotten away. Jane had successfully put Garrett to bed and was busy throwing clothes in the wash. It was 9:00 P.M. and I was longing for a good night's rest. It was good to be home.

The phone rang and I ran to answer it. It was Jim Gritter and his news was astounding. We had been chosen by Jennifer, a young mother from the Detroit area. She had a one-month-old boy and was looking forward to meeting us. Jim suggested we give her a call since she was eager to hear from us.

Several minutes passed as we let this news sink in. This was not exactly a routine phone call. What does one say? In fact, how does one even start the conversation? Not exactly sure how to proceed, we dialed the number and hoped for the best. Fortunately conversation came easily to us, and quickly plans to visit her were in place. Jennifer seemed so pleasant that by the time our chat ended, we felt we had made a friend. Wild with excitement, we took turns calling family and friends. What an evening! A lot of living had gone into the past hour.

Two days later we were sitting in Jennifer's living room. As public schoolteachers, meetings are an everyday fact of life for us, but those meetings hardly equip a person for this kind of encounter, and we were nervous. It's amazing how these experiences seem so nerve-racking as they are anticipated and so wonderful as they are recalled. We had brought along Garrett and he did a wonderful job as an icebreaker. Jennifer's mom and Jim both contributed to the discussion also. Jennifer explained that she had been thinking about adoption for a long time and while she was still pregnant had made plans with another agency. She said they had promised openness but they seemed very unsure of themselves. Jennifer noted that she lost confidence in that organization and didn't trust their ability to make effective arrangements.

During her pregnancy she was staying with some caring foster parents, Alice and Grant Rath. They had told her about Community, Family and Children Services and that is how Jennifer had learned about us. She told us that she had selected us from a number of prospects because of our strong religious convictions and our positive attitude towards openness. As the meeting went on, it was clear to us that Jennifer approved of us. She had strong feelings about bringing the baby to us, so a plan was established which called for her to retrieve the baby from foster care on Saturday, three days later, and bring him the many miles to our house. That sounded great to us, and we left the meeting full of excitement. We spent most of our trip home marveling at the composure and dignity of this remarkable young lady.

We could hardly wait for the three days to pass. Finally the designated time arrived and we had supper ready. The phone rang and we were informed that their departure had been delayed, but that they were on their way and would join us in a couple of hours. This was to be our first contact with our new son, and further delay seemed unbearable. Finally the car pulled into our long driveway and we welcomed them into the house. At last it was time for us to meet the baby. Just like in the movies, it was love at first sight! He was very handsome with dark hair, dark blue eyes, and a round chubby face. We were hooked.

We spent the evening in pleasant, relaxed conversation and used the occasion to get to know each other better. The Raths joined us later on, and we were pleased to meet them since they had been so good to Jennifer. On parting, we made plans to meet again the next day.

Sunday we tackled the challenge of supplying our little boy a name. Jennifer, Jane, and I each shared several ideas before we collectively settled on Aaron Alex. The naming process symbolized our determination to work together in Aaron's behalf. The weekend drew to a close and the moment of leaving was tender and sad. It is powerful consolation to know that the goodbyes are not forever.

Jennifer has returned to our house for three different weekends. We have met her brother and sister since each of them took a turn driving her up to see us. We also met Jennifer at the bus station for one trip. She fits into our home beautifully and we look forward to her visits. Both of the boys respond to her very well as she has an excellent way with children. We have visited with Jennifer at the Raths and have been to her home three different times. We usually leave Aaron with Jennifer for the day while we visit friends in the area. We are very relaxed in leaving Aaron with her because we know she will be an exceptionally attentive baby-sitter. On the average, Aaron and Jennifer have gotten together about every other month since they joined our family.

We cannot begin to describe our affection for Jennifer. Although she is young, she is unusually mature and has a loving and caring personality. She has become a valued and respected part of our family. We love her and we love our son. We look forward to a lifetime of loving and sharing the joy of Aaron. Perhaps open adoption has seen finer moments than what we have experienced with Jennifer, but it's hard for us to imagine. Jennifer took a difficult situation and created something beautiful from it. We think that as God looks down on Jennifer, He has lots of reasons to smile.

Gloria and Andy Thomas

"A whole different perspective"

"**I** want twelve children!" I can still hear myself telling Andy this on the night we announced our engagement. I was partly serious—in a spontaneous sort of way. I knew I definitely wanted a large family. Whether twelve was the optimum number remained to be seen. My judgment was slightly colored by the fact that I had just returned from living in Spain for ten years where most of my friends came from families of ten or more while I was an only child.

I am thankful I had the presence of mind to relay this desire to Andy while he was sitting down, with me on his lap. To say the least, he was stunned and made a more realistic count of three to four children. In my mind I thought, "We'll see about that," and we happily proceeded to draw up a list of names we both liked. One thing for certain, we both liked children. That very night was our first family-planning discussion.

Nine years later we adopted David. It was a long road to that day. Hard, lonely, frustrating in the effort to conceive, but filled with years of enjoying ourselves without the responsibility of children. It was longer than we wished it to be, but infertility is a condition that is hard to accept. With the medical advances of today one cannot believe there is not a cure or help. We began to talk about adoption three to four years before we got David. I am glad now that we did not immediately act on the thought because we might not have heard about CFCS or open adoption.

When we finally did decide to adopt, it was a weight off our shoulders. We called the agency and inquired about their program. I tried to make my voice sound like the perfect adoptive voice when all the time I wanted to shout at Jim over the phone, "When can we meet? Give me baby figures! If you have a baby there now, we'll take it!" We were ready. But as in most things in the adult world, one must wait patiently. At least that's what we thought at the time.

The meetings were exciting. There we were, sitting with "the group" of potential adoptive parents. Our eyes scanned the crowd while we rated our chances. One of my fears was that the agency would find us unacceptable but Jim eased my mind by saying that the group looked strong and they would probably be able to work with us all. That was a relief. I could relax a little. One cannot possible realize the emotional pressure involved and this would be nothing compared to being chosen, meeting the birthmother, and taking the baby home.

With the homestudy and preparatory group meetings behind us, we turned in our portfolio of information which the agency uses to acquaint birthparents with prospective families. Now the grueling wait would begin.

Twelve days later Chris phoned. I was home alone when the call came. Even though we had been forewarned that we might be receiving an important call, I was shocked. I distinctly remember hearing, yet not hearing her. She told me her name (which luckily I already knew or I might not have believed her), and that she chose us to have her baby. She also hit me with the bombshell that she was going to see the doctor because she was feeling different; she was beginning to experience early signs of labor. If the baby were to arrive now, it would be three weeks earlier than the doctor predicted. She said she would call us up when she got back early that afternoon.

I do not need to tell you my excitement! I immediately called Andy. This was the start of what was to become our most incredible weekend ever. At 2 o'clock she called back and said that the doctor advised her not to travel—that she could have her baby at any minute, or up to a week. Her original plans were to deliver the baby in Grand Rapids where she was living at the time. Instead, she found herself visiting her grandparents in Cadillac, her hometown. We were all excited about the news and tried to get acquainted over the phone.

Returning from a Christmas party that evening, we called Chris in hope of getting to know her a little better. Her mother answered the phone by saying that Chris was finally resting, and during that brief conversation Chris came downstairs and told her mom—and us indirectly—that her water had broken and asked to be taken to the hospital. We felt like we were there! We quickly hung up, saying that we would call tomorrow morning to see what had happened.

It was a long night. We were two hours away and we did not know what to do or what to expect. The next morning, we drove into Traverse City to see Jim at the agency. We all decided that he should call the hospital and talk to Chris to see how she felt, if she had had the baby yet, and if she wanted us to come down. It was like being on trial and waiting for the verdict to come in. Jim called her grandparents' house and got her grandfather. We listened to his side of the conversation. "Oh, a little boy." Andy and I looked at one another; he had tears in his eyes; he really wanted a boy. Then Jim chuckled, "Hands like a gorilla!" We got the hospital number from him and then called Chris. The baby was born early that morning—4:47 A.M., weighed 8 lbs., 14 oz., and was 22½ inches long. A big, healthy boy! But the best news was that she still wanted us to come down and meet her and get to know the baby.

Our main conversation on the way to the hospital was about names. We had not thought of any and the list we made nine years ago was long lost. It was made easier by the fact that we had only to decide on a boy's name.

The closer we got to Cadillac, the more nervous we became. Jim told us before we left that ideally the birth and adoptive parents should meet before the birth and in a place more familiar and comfortable than a hospital. So there we were, walking into a hospital, having only talked to Chris a total of twenty minutes on the phone and she just having delivered a baby and most likely feeling very tired and sore. Neither Chris nor we had had a chance to adjust to each other. We had not the slightest idea what she looked like nor she us. Because the baby came early, Chris had only seen photocopied pictures of us which had been mailed to her. Fortunately those obscure grey pictures, accompanied by our written material, had caught her attention. All we knew about her was from Jim—that she was cute, warm, gregarious, and that he would welcome her into his family any day. That was more than good enough for us!

Cadillac has a small community hospital. As I mentioned, Chris grew up there, so we realized that we could be walking into a hostile environment. Who wants to see a native daughter with strong family ties give her baby up to total strangers? In the end, though, Cadillac proved to be everything but hostile. We were allowed to go into the hospital whenever we wanted and to hold the baby. We were made to feel part of the family.

We walked into the hospital, found the maternity ward, and passed the nursery. There were three babies and I saw that the cutest one had Chris' name on his bed. We did not stay there long, though we wanted to. There were several strange and awkward moments throughout, and this was one of them. We would have liked to spend several minutes just staring at him and talking about "our new son" but it was a little early for that. We were ushered into a room by the nurse who said we would have more privacy here and that she would get Chris and her mom. We were obviously expected.

It was perfect immediately. Chris and her mom walked in and we hugged each other. We congratulated Chris on her delivery and then sat down. Chris lay down on a nearby bed and we began to talk. Our first impression of her was that she was very pretty, but she did not feel so and was worried that she looked awful. During that time, we got some family background about Chris, her parents, and about the birthfather, and they got some information from us. We discovered that the birthfather was not a factor in her decision and that she had not been seeing him for months. You could tell, though, that there were still strong feelings in the relationship. We told Chris that we expected her to be very present in the baby's life and that he should get to know her well. We were all for a very open relationship. After a while, she asked us if we wanted to see and hold the baby. We scrubbed, put on some gowns, and proceeded to fall in love with him right away. I am amazed how quickly bonding happened. Already we could not imagine our lives without him.

Chris was getting tired so we decided to go. Her mother then invited us to meet some more of the family. She warned us of her father (Chris' grandfather)—that he was big and gruff and would probably ask us a lot of questions, especially about religion. If we did not let him "get to us," we would get along great. With that brief preparation, we set off to meet them. They made us feel at home right away and her dad was like a big stuffed bear; we liked them immediately. Dorothy, Chris' grandmother, said that I reminded her of Chris, which I took as a compliment, and Don, her grandfather, said that he was glad we were the ones to get the baby. One of the remarkable features of this family was their height. Chris is the shortest in her immediate family at 5′8″. Her mother is 6′ tall, her brother is 6′7″, her grandmother is 6′, and so on. So after meeting all these great tall people, we sat down to a big dinner, stopped briefly back at the hospital, and drove home feeling great.

We called Chris Sunday morning to see how she was feeling and what her thoughts were about us today. We were totally unprepared for her answer. She said that she was not as sure as before and that she did not know what to tell us about coming down. She did not want us to get any more attached to the baby in case she changed her mind, yet realized that it was important for us to be there if she did not.

We were a mess! We immediately called Jim, packed a suitcase, and left for Traverse City and booked a motel room for the day. We had to get out of the house. We called Jim again. He had talked to Chris and said he had a hard time reading her but suggested that we go down and see her. It was a touchy time. If we made ourselves too scarce, it could be seen as disinterest. On the other hand, if we were too visible, it might be viewed as pressure. We decided that if we were going to err, it should certainly not be in the direction of disinterest, for we most definitely were interested. So down we went for a long two-and-a-half-hour drive. We were in dread . . .

We peered into Chris' room and found her in bed, with her mom holding the baby. She thanked us for coming, and said that they were trying to decide what was best for the child. We agreed, told them not to worry about our feelings if she changed her mind, and that a right decision without our pressure was what she needed. She asked us if we wanted to hold him once more. It was so painful just standing there in the doorway that we declined and left.

For Chris, a lot of things were happening. Her decision to give up the baby with such assurance was changed once the baby arrived. She was also being confronted by different members of her family who urged her to keep him in the family until she was ready to take care of him. What we were going through was nothing compared to her ordeal. She told us later that there were two reasons she remained with her original decision. One was that one of the nurses at the hospital and a close friend of the family told Chris to try to remember her reasons for choosing adoption during the last nine months and not to become clouded by the last two days. The other was that she really wanted him to have a father. Her own parents were divorced.

On Monday morning Chris called Andy at our woodworking shop. She told him that she had decided to go through with the adoption and to come by early Tuesday morning when she was to be released, and be ready to pick up the baby. We were awake by 3:30 A.M., drove in to Traverse City to pick up Jim who was coming with us, and were in Cadillac by 8:30. Chris did a good job of masking her obvious pain. She seemed very excited for us and watched us dress him and take over the parent role. We told her that we had decided on the name "David" and she asked if we had a middle name picked out yet. We did not, and she thought she would like to leave him something of herself, suggesting Christopher. We agreed right away.

When we finally had David dressed and ready to go. Chris briefly touched his hair ever so gently and so full of love. It was a poignant moment—one I never will forget. The last image that day was of us all getting into our cars, us driving north to a new life with David, and Chris and her mother driving south without him. I had a distinct feeling, at that moment, of having stolen this child away. It colored my excitement and enhanced my feelings toward Chris for weeks to come. I saw her every time I looked at him and just marveled at the open adoption process. Even though there is a lot of pain in the open adoption method, I cannot imagine not being part of this incredible experience. It gives you a whole different perspective than if you just received your baby six weeks to two months later from a foster parent.

That was 22 months ago. Chris is now a junior in college and helping at a pre-school in Ann Arbor. She is still seeing the birth-father, though their relationship is a stormy one. We have had Chris up for eight or ten weekends so far, some including her mother. It is fun having her around. She still tells us how glad she is with the decision she made. She says the pain is gone and she is happy that it is all behind her now. She is very smart and self-assured. You know exactly what is on her mind.

David hit the terrible twos about a year ago. We do a lot of running after him. It is "I want" one moment and "No, I don't want" the next. He started talking at eleven months and has not stopped since. He is extremely bright and determined to get his own way. He cannot sit still for a minute, unless he is sick. He does like to kiss, though. He looks just like Chris did at that age. There is a little of us coming through in him, though. The way he says, "Andy" when he wants something from him . . . Andy says it sounds just like me. After a hard day of romping around the house at full speed, David enjoys some manly time with his father. That puts him on a parallel track with his dad who enjoys nothing more than some exclusive time with his son after a hard day of work.

And Andy and I? We love to watch him. Andy's standard daily question is, "Can you believe how beautiful he is? He's my boy!" So now, depending on who you talk to, it's one down and three to go . . . or is it eleven?

Dawn and Dave Ehle

"Love is patient"

"I'm sorry but there is very little hope that you will ever be able to have children. There is nothing that can be done medically." What a blow to receive after so much testing and in some cases pain. We had always expected to have children . . . it was part of our "plan": 2.7 children, a stable income, and a place in the country (although we might skip the white picket fence).

We entered a quiet grief period for the children we would never hold or see grow. For the questions that would go unanswered: What would the child look like? How would it behave? On and on, but now these questions and feelings had to be dealt with. Obviously God did not intend for us to have children. Perhaps some day we would understand the reason, perhaps not.

So now the next question, did God want us to have a family at all? We both felt very strongly that He did and would provide a way of forming this family. We began looking into different avenues for beginning our family: foreign adoption, foster parenting, special needs children, and traditional infant adoption. After much soul searching, we decided that we really wanted to adopt an infant.

At that time, we lived in southern Michigan and we began to investigate all the adoption agencies serving our area. Most said we would have to wait four to nine years and could adopt only one child; some were not accepting any more names. This news was another blow.

About a year later we relocated to northern Michigan where we came into contact with the Community, Family and Children Services (CFCS) and open adoption. Jim Gritter explained the philosophy and said that we could adopt more that one child. Best of all, the process usually occurred in less that one year—unbelievable and a true answer to prayer!

The first step was the orientation meeting. We were a little skeptical of openness but felt more comfortable after this meeting. Next came the three educational meetings. These were really interesting although they made us a little apprehensive. It felt like we were competing with the other couples for a limited number of children. Dave and I decided to become radicals and ask the unpopular but essential questions: "What if the child is seriously handicapped, mentally retarded, or we don't want to be chosen by a particular birthmother?" No one wanted to ask; it might look like you would settle for perfection and nothing less. That wasn't our reason; we just wanted to be ready for any complications that might arise.

To answer our questions Jim explained that if a child was born with medical complications we could obtain financial assistance for medical expenses. Jim also explained we could refuse to accept a child or a birthmother but he had never seen that happen.

The "one on two" sessions with Jim soon followed. We really enjoyed these because we discussed subjects which are typically put off until you're in the middle of the situation. The meetings also helped us define how we felt about open adoption, how our families would react, and the type of relationship we wanted with the birthfamily. In conjunction with these meetings, we were making our photo album. Our goal was to portray the true "us" so that similar birthparents would pick us. The project was time-consuming but fun.

Finally, all the paperwork and interviews were done. It was the beginning of March, 1985. Now the wait began. Every time the phone rang we hoped it was Jim bringing good news. We heard other couples were chosen before us and wondered what was so great about "them", weren't we okay too? We really felt that we were in a strange kind of competition and had just gotten passed over!

Time helped us understand how this match-up worked for everyone's best interest.

Near mid-April I was raking the lawn when the phone rang. It was Jim. "You've been chosen," he said. It was a wonderful moment. I asked when the birthmother was due and he said she already had given birth two days earlier and it was a boy! I was so excited I had to call Dave at work and let him know. Dave yelled it out so everyone at the office shared the news.

To make a long story shorter, this potential adoption fell through. The birthmother changed her mind and we took the baby back to the agency after one day at home. We had not had time to become very attached to the baby, but we had never been through anything as difficult. We had been so thrilled to finally be parents and establishing our family. It seemed as though all was lost and we were back to square one.

Six weeks later we were chosen again. This time it was a couple that chose us and they were five months along. That meant we had substantially more time to get to know each other and we used the time well. We became close friends with these impressive young people and shared weekly letters, phone calls, and visits with them. We all wanted the pregnancy to go well and we did whatever we could to further that goal. We were having the time of our lives!

At the end of September, a gorgeous baby boy was born. We opened our hearts and our home to him, and two weeks into our relationship we would have walked through fire for him. In a sense we did, because it was at that point that the birthparents called to tell us they had changed their minds.

This was devastating. We were attached to this baby and we each handled the grief our own way. Dave plunged into work and simply stated, "This is God's will, even though we don't understand why." I wasn't working so I couldn't help but dwell on it. I felt filled with anger, which was a type of defense to see me through the rough water. I put the baby clothes away and got out of our house for a couple of days. I cried the 145 miles to my parent's house. This was a gash that took months to truly heal to the point of forgiveness.

At this point we wondered if we should try again. We began looking at other agencies which didn't have this risk associated with them. Our families were also grieving and questioning our participation in open adoption/foster parenting. We decided we did want to know the birthfamily and to give it three strikes before we'd get out.

One month after we took the second baby back, we received a call from a girl named Dawn (could it be mere coincidence that we shared the same name?) saying she had chosen us as parents for her baby which was due in two and a half months. We were cautiously hopeful. It was hard to believe that anyone would follow through with their plans. Dawn explained her reasons for deciding on adoption and it sounded almost too familiar.

We went down to Dawn's house to meet her and her family. One thing we soon came to realize about Dawn was her total honesty and conviction about what she was doing. She said what she thought—not because it sounded mature or because it might be what we wanted to hear, but because of the way she felt.

After the initial visit we would talk on the phone and write. This was important for all of us. We knew the hospital setting would be uncomfortable but getting to know each other beforehand would ease some of this tension.

Dawn called us when she went into labor so we jumped in the car to try and get there in time. Dawn had asked if I wanted to be in the delivery room with her but the hospital staff wouldn't include me. (It was their first open adoption situation and they were very uncomfortable with it.)

That afternoon, Dawn delivered a healthy boy. We saw him about one and a half hours after birth and were excited and scared at the same time. Trying to hold back our feelings wouldn't work—we knew that from experience—so we decided we would be excited, and if things didn't work out we'd just have to survive it once again.

We named the baby Daniel James, and Dawn put that name along with our last name on the birth certificate. That amazed us. We were surprised she was so very sure of her decision. Dawn kept reassuring us that she was not going to change her mind, but I guess we didn't look 100% confident. She did not hold Daniel or feed him because she felt this would build a bond that was not wise to build.

Taking Daniel from the hospital was a very emotional time. Dawn's parents were having difficulty letting go but Dawn was very strong and confident throughout. We felt such admiration for her. She had no doubts that her decision was best for the baby and for her also. We just hoped she would continue this way through all the court proceedings.

We took Daniel home and he captured our hearts. He was a good sleeper and eater with an even disposition. Dawn and her family stopped by after signing the court papers and appreciated seeing where Daniel would be raised. It was a happy, warm, and close get-together and they inspired confidence when they said, "This will be a great place for Daniel to grow up and you will be super parents."

Daniel is now 8 months old and we have seen Dawn and her family twice since they stopped by after signing the court papers. We appreciate Dawn more than we ever thought we would. Dawn has said she has never regretted her decision and views us as Daniel's mom and dad. This was a point we always wondered about. Would the birthmother feel like the "real" mom and expect to be treated as such?

In our eyes Dawn is a very close friend and we want it to remain that way. We are very interested in how she is doing and feel comfortable talking with her. This was a surprise. We thought it would be awkward and we would feel defensive. Dawn is everything we had hoped for in a birthmother. Open adoption has been a successful option for her and for us.

As for Daniel, we cannot imagine life without him. We would go through all the tears and heartache of the last year again for our little guy. We once wondered if we could really love a child adopted into our family as much as one born to us. That question has been answered. We have dreams, hopes, and endless love for our son. God has provided a way for us to have a family—our prayers are answered.

In a year or so we will return to the CFCS agency in hopes of adopting a second child. And we will gladly bear the risks of taking a baby home from the hospital and having a birthmother change her mind. It isn't easy to go through, but we have learned that the benefits far outweigh the risks and that God knows what He is doing.

Mike and Jean Spry—III

"Good things come"

In this chapter, Mike writes of the third experience he and Jean had with openness in adoption.

The voice on the other end of the phone was unmistakable—it was Abbie Nelson. " . . . Where are you going to be tomorrow?"

"I'll be home with Lara all day."

"Now I don't want you to get excited or anything," there was a definite note of caution in Abbie's voice, "but I'd like you guys to be *ready* tomorrow."

"What do you mean by *ready*, Abbie; are you saying that a baby could be released to us tomorrow?"

"Well, that's a possibility, but I don't want you and Jean to get excited or anything."

My mind raced with speculation. I knew that the agency was very busy with new referrals; there had recently been an article on the agency's adoption program in the Sunday supplement of the *Detroit News* and it had generated a lot of interest. I wondered if this referral had resulted from the article, if perhaps it was one of those "lightning bolt" placements that seem to come from out of nowhere when a birthmother finds out about the program at the very end of her pregnancy. It was time to go fishing for additional clues.

"Abbie, is this a referral that came as a result of the article?"

"Yes."

"Is this birthmother out of town?"

"Yes."

"About how far away?"

"It's about a three-hour drive."

"And the baby has been born and could be released tomorrow?"

"That's a possibility, but I don't want you guys to get excited. I *do* want you to be *ready* tomorrow, though, just in case." Abbie clearly wanted to give out no more information than was absolutely necessary to insure our readiness. I told her that I would do my best to follow her advice.

Be ready, but don't get excited—what conflicting dynamics! This advice would have been difficult to follow a few months earlier—before our experience with Jesse and his family; it now seemed a very prudent course to bridle our optimism and exercise a full measure of denial. We were now well aware that premature excitement could lead to a great deal of pain. We would simply have to deal with the next day as though it was an ordinary one and do the bare minimum to get ready; this would help to minimize our emotional investment.

If I didn't permit myself the luxury of optimism, I did indulge heavily in conjecture—reading between the lines of my conversation with Abbie. It appeared that this was a situation where the birthmother had given birth before either Jim or Abbie could get fully acquainted with her. She had probably chosen us tentatively, based on limited information. I was betting that Abbie had alerted us based on this tentative selection, but that she planned to more thoroughly analyze the birthmother's situation and present her with more detailed information on available adoptive couples before finalizing any decisions. If the birthmother was firm in her resolve to release, if she still wanted us after looking through all of the files, and if Abbie was comfortable with everything, we would get "the call." It logically followed that Abbie would want us to be ready in case the preliminary plan went forward, but in recognizing the great likelihood that everything could collapse when more complete information was gathered, she wanted us to "not get too excited"—she didn't want us to get hurt again.

The next twenty-four hours were a bit strange. Both Jean and I tried to go about our business as usual. Oh, there were some additional activities—boiling nipples, buying diapers and sleepers, packing diaper bags, etc.—but all were done in a stupor of denial, simply pretending that there was nothing unusual about doing any of these things on this particular day. Each task was approached in a calm, matter-of-fact manner and blended in with our typical daily patterns. We were fully prepared for the day to come and go without hearing a word from the agency.

The call from Abbie came at about 2:15 P.M. She was in Lansing with a birthmother named Amy. Amy got on the phone and said that she was very anxious to meet us and have us see *our new son*. "Oh my," I thought, as my mental processes shifted into overdrive. After expressing my pleasure with her selection of us, I made arrangements for Jean, Lara, and me to meet her and the baby that evening.

Before Jean got home to pick up Lara and me for the trip, Abbie called with some additional information; on the whole she confirmed most of my speculations. She had met with Amy that morning for the first time after bringing down several files for her to examine. Amy had learned of the program through the *Detroit News* article and planned to contact the agency before the baby was born. Because she suddenly delivered six weeks prematurely, however, Amy wasn't able to talk with Abbie until the day after the birth. She initially selected us over the phone after Abbie had read a number of "three-page summaries" written by adoptive couples. Amy had insisted that Abbie get in touch with us so that we could be ready if the baby was released the next day. Thus came the original call telling us to be ready. As it turned out, we would not need to be quite so ready yet; the baby could not come home with us for at least another day. Although he was a large 'preemie' (5lb., 10 oz.) and in generally good health, he was still on oxygen and was being tube-fed.

After getting the basic information from Abbie and Amy, we left for Lansing. Our use of denial throughout the day had been so expert that we were both having trouble turning it off on the way down. Could we actually be traveling to meet the mother of our soon-to-be-adopted son? Somehow the whole situation didn't seem real—it still felt like an ordinary day. We busied ourselves by discussing names and talking with Lara about what was to come. It wasn't until we hit the city limits of East Lansing that the adrenalin started to flow.

That evening we not only met Amy, but her mother, sister, and five-month-old nephew, as well. They all seemed to be very receptive toward us and the whole concept of openness in adoption; we were given a very warm welcome. We talked at length about our previous experience with the program and about their hopes and expectations for our relationship. We were pleased to find out that they all wanted to maintain contact.

Amy told us that she had been working with another agency throughout her pregnancy and had sought the opportunity to choose the adoptive couple and meet with them before the birth. The social worker had told her that this was not possible in the State of Michigan and Amy had resigned herself to experiencing the depression that usually goes along with releasing a baby through traditional adoption—sadness on birthdays and holidays, persistent wondering about the child's well-being and whereabouts, etc.

Miraculously, Amy's father had seen the article in the *Detroit News* and immediately sent a copy to her. Before she could contact the agency, she went into labor, and the baby got an early start on life. When Amy called Abbie after the baby was born, she thought it would be too late for the agency to consider arranging an open adoption. She was pleasantly surprised to find that it was hardly too late. Abbie immediately questioned her about what she was looking for in a couple, read some summaries from relevant files, and, as fate would have it, she chose us. One day later, here we were in her apartment. Throughout our conversation, Amy kept saying, "I can't believe this is happening!" She seemed to be so surprised and delighted that she could be such a welcome part of her baby's life. A mutual admiration society developed quickly; it was not hard to see that Amy was a very special young lady with a caring heart and that she had the support of a loving family.

We asked about the baby's birthfather. Amy informed us that

his name was Dan and that he was a farmer. He was not yet aware that the baby had been born because he had gone on vacation and she was unable to reach him. She expressed her feeling that Dan would probably go along with the adoption as they had discussed, although she didn't feel she could guarantee that he would stay in that frame of mind once he saw his new son. Amy hoped that we would take the baby home in spite of the risk that Dan could change his mind afterward. We said that we would take that chance to insure early bonding between us and the baby.

Excitedly, we met Amy, her mother, and Abbie at the hospital to see the baby for the first time. He was still on oxygen in the isolette and we were only allowed to touch him through the portholes. The poor little guy had tubes running in and out of him, but nonetheless was as cute as could be. He was so tiny! Each of us took a turn at stroking him as we all marveled at this incredible little boy.

Amy had not yet named him because she wanted his adoptive parents to do it. We told her that our preference was that we all name him jointly, that his name would be that much more special and meaningful if it came from all of us. We must have kicked around names for 45 minutes, easily resolving that Amy's last name would be the baby's middle name, but having trouble with the rest. Every name that someone promoted generated an objection by someone else. Jean finally had to take our restless two-year-old out into the hallway for a little energy dissipation.

When we all reconvened, Abbie said that they had come up with a few more ideas. The first name that came out of her mouth was "Ian." I laughed out loud and threw my hands into the air. This was a name I had lobbied for over the last several months throughout the many discussions Jean and I had about names. Jean liked the name very much, but had some strong reservations about it because we had once named a pet Ian. We had always resolved (and reaffirmed this on our way to Lansing) that neither of us would ever bring the name up with a birthparent, but if it was suggested by someone else, we would earnestly consider it. Clearly it was meant to be. Everybody liked "Ian" as a first name and so that is what he became. Amy sat in disbelief, she was so amazed and very pleased that we wanted her to participate fully in the naming of her baby. And we were delighted that Ian had gotten his name from all of us.

Before we all left, the nurses informed us that the baby would probably not go home for a few days, and we decided that we would return to Interlochen immediately so that we could have a chance to tie up some very loose ends. We said that we wanted to spend one day getting things ready at home and come back to Lansing on the following day regardless of whether the discharge was planned.

Thus began a week of complete and utter exhaustion. One day we would make the 180-mile trip to Lansing, spend time with Ian and Amy, then drive back to Interlochen; the next day we would get things in order on the home front and in our jobs in case the baby came home on the following day. In all, we made five trips to Lansing over a nine-day period—over 1800 miles in all.

On our second trip, we met Dan and Ben, Ian's birthfather and half-brother. Dan was rather surprised to return from vacation and find himself invited over to Amy's apartment to meet the baby's adoptive parents. After getting acquainted with Ben and Dan at the apartment, we joined them and Amy at the hospital nursery. I had to resist a great deal of temptation to run in and simply pick up Ian; I felt that Dan should have the first opportunity to hold him. Each of us took our turn with Ian while he was out of the isolette and many memorable photos were taken. At one point I got a chance to talk with Dan alone and asked him how he felt about the whole arrangement. He shrugged and said that he would go along with the adoption as Amy wished. I explained our will-ingness to be open and stay in touch. He thanked me, but said we probably wouldn't hear from him more than once a year.

It was clear by the end of this trip that Ian would not be going home for at least three more days. He was under the bilirubin light and was having trouble with nipple feeding after being tube-fed in the early going. It was almost scary the first time we fed him—his suck was incredibly feeble and it took over an hour of coaxing to get 1½ ounces of formula into him. Everyone assured us, however, that this was common in premature infants and we observed steady progress each time we saw him.

Ian's long hospitalization seemed to take its toll on Amy. Each time we saw her it appeared as though the situation was weighing more heavily on her. I don't think it was a matter of changing her mind about the release for she always seemed firm in her resolve; she just seemed to be more acutely aware with each passing day of how difficult the release would be. What made the anticipation of the release even harder was that the hospital would not allow Ian to be discharged to us as foster parents. Amy would have to hand the baby over to us. She knew this would be a very emotional moment. Although the period of hospitalization was difficult, it at least served the purpose of drawing everyone closer together through the time that we shared.

When Ian was nine days old, plans were made to release him on the following day. Amy, Jean, and I spent time with the baby and met his pediatrician to discuss Ian's health needs. The final diagnosis was a simple one, but the words were wonderful—"normal, healthy baby boy." We began to make our plans for the discharge. We all agreed that Amy would come up to the hospital at 4 P.M. the next day to spend some time with Ian and get him ready to leave. We would bring the car-seat and his clothing up to the nursery and wait in the lobby until 5 P.M. Amy would simply hand the baby to us and walk away without exchanging any words; she felt it would be too difficult to do it any other way. We readily understood.

The next day everything went pretty much according to plan until the "eleventh hour" when some unnecessary fumbling on the part of hospital staff caused a significant delay. However, Amy was feeling better than she expected, according to her mother, and would spend some time with us before we all left. The actual release was kind of awkward, but perhaps they all are. You want to say something profound and comforting, but no words seem to suffice. We were looking for Amy to get off one of the public elevators we had been using all week, but all of a suddenly I looked up, and there were Amy, her mother, and Ian. They had taken a staff elevator along with a nurse and seemingly came from out of nowhere, catching me completely unprepared. I felt like I had two left feet.

Amy asked Lara if she wanted to see her new little brother and I walked her over to see the baby. Jean hugged Amy and said, "Thanks for trusting us"—the very words I had in mind, leaving me with nothing to say. All I could do was give Amy a hug and stand dumbfounded, groping for some appropriate words. There seemed to be no good way to say goodbye; there was so much love and concern present at that moment, but nobody could find the means to express it adequately. Jean handed Amy's mom the small gift we had gotten for Amy (a birthstone pendant) and they made their farewell.

Jean brought the car while I talked to the attending nurse and watched Lara and Ian. We loaded up and found a card from Amy in the car-seat with Ian. As we started back toward Interlochen with our new family member, I opened the card and slowly read it aloud to Jean.

Because I have a fear of not being able to say a proper good-bye to you on this happy, yet sad, day, I wanted to say a few things in a short letter.

First of all, thank you so much for all the love, support, and care you have given Ian and I this past week. It has meant a whole bunch! I just couldn't get through this if you weren't both such wonderful people!

I wish you the best with your new son. I will certainly miss him with all my heart, but I will make it knowing he is with you being well taken care of, and best of all "happy!"

Ian is your son now, knowing that he is with you will make my days go on. I'm happy for you and I'm very happy for Ian!

Thank you for being the lovely people you are. I pray Ian grows up to be just like you!

I truly love you with all my heart! Take care. And have a safe trip home!

> *Love you*
> *Amy*

We drove on with tears in our eyes and in our hearts.

Epilogue

In the 2½ months since Ian's birth, Amy has visited on three occasions, bringing both friends and family members with her. We are looking forward to having a warm, loving, and very open relationship with her and the people in her life. It feels so good to be able to give her something back for the incredible gift she has shared with us. We were also both surprised and pleased to receive an early visit from Dan and Ben. Both have decided that they, too, want to maintain ongoing contact. Dan, in fact, had already started a picture book.

Everything appears to be in place for some rewarding future experiences with our birthfamilies—experiences that should enrich Ian's life and all of our lives beyond measure—all due to a very special program that brings people *together* rather than separating them *forever*.

Afterword

The action in these stories typically begins with the stunning intru-
sion of "The Call" into the placid, well-ordered existence of a
prospective adoptive family. That call, informing the family that
they have been selected to receive a child, is a watershed event
which forever changes their lives. For them, all that really matters
are the events which follow. The reader, however, will sense that
some significant preparations preceded that dramatic call, and will
likely be curious about those preparations. It is well, then, to briefly touch on the agency's efforts to equip the families for the remarkable drama of open adoption.

The stories more accurately begin with a call that these aspir-
ing adoptive parents have made themselves. They contacted Community, Family and Children Services, the social service arm of
the Catholic Diocese of Gaylord (Michigan), to research their
prospects for adoption. The callers quickly learned that the agency
has an unusual approach to adoption. In order to participate in
this program, they should not only be prepared to be selected by
the birthparents, but also be ready to meet them and enter a
meaningful relationship with them. They are then given a brief
synopsis of how the program operates.

Callers are typically astonished to discover how elaborate the
process is and will likely view the idea of openness with skepticism. Initial responses to open adoption tend to be quite emotional

and range from outright revulsion to enthusiastic delight. The majority of inquirers respond with uncertainty and ambivalence.

The educational process

The process we describe to them may sound almost like an obstacle course. It begins with eight hours of education in a group format to acquaint them with the rationale for open adoption followed by a two-hour meeting with just the two of them. At that point both they and the agency have to make a decision as to whether or not to proceed. If both sides agree to press on, they begin the home study phase which is composed of five private counseling sessions covering such issues as motivation, personal development, marriage, parenting style, and attitudes toward adoption. It is in these sessions that we try to become better acquainted with each couple so that we can assess their readiness for open adoption.

Once the home study is complete, the educational process resumes with five more group meetings. This time the meetings are rotated among the homes of the various group members and as a result the tone of the meetings becomes more relaxed, sometimes even festive. Frequently the couples continue to meet long after the agency ceases its direct involvement. The support derived from these groups can help sustain couples as they enter the most taxing phase of the experience—waiting.

While it may seem that a great deal of time is spent in this educational effort, it is necessary since there is much material to cover. Over the several sessions, the classes will examine at least three major areas. First of all, they will critique the confidential system of adoption. Second, they will identify the unique advantages of the open approach. Third, for the purpose of presenting a balanced perspective, the classes will wrestle with the hazards attendant upon open adoption. These are crucial subjects which merit careful consideration.

As important as this educational material is, it is secondary to the enthusiasm of the presenter. The receptivity of the prospective adoptive parents to these new ideas is directly correlated to the confidence and conviction that the professional has in this philosophy. If the presenter is not well-grounded in these concepts, seems unsure, or appears to go along with the idea begrudgingly, a response of diminished expectations, fearfulness, and resistance is likely.

Problems of the closed adoption system

Since most people have at least a general understanding of the *closed* adoption system, the educational process begins by assessing that approach. While it is conceded that the old system worked reasonably well for many people, it is also noted that the system is far from perfect and has inadvertently claimed many victims, particularly among birthparents and adoptees. Closed adoption is criticized for three major shortcomings: its commitment to secrecy, its poor handling of vital information, and its insistence on retaining complete control over the experience.

1. The heart of the problem with confidential adoption is its affection for and dependence on secrecy. Originally intended to protect adoptees, birthparents, and adoptive parents from the stigmas of illegitimacy, out of wedlock pregnancy, and infertility, secrecy has outlived its utility as our society has become increasingly nonchalant about such things. Ironically, secrecy tends to shroud adoption with unwholesome connotations and now creates the very aura of illegitimacy that it was intended to overcome. Sadly, secrecy begets an atmosphere in which fear thrives. Creative energy is tragically siphoned off in the endless effort to sustain the secrets. Even if secrecy was desirable, it is an illusion since it cannot actually be maintained. Mary Jo Rillera, founder of a major resource center for searchers called the Triadoption Library, has stated that ninety percent of those persons who earnestly search will find. That simple observation single-handedly demolishes the viability of confidential adoption.

The choice facing adoptive parents, then, is between a system which is obsolete, counter-productive, illusory, and inextricably tied to fear . . . or an approach which features openness and candor.

2. A second major flaw in the confidential system is the awkward

manner in which it gathers and transmits information. The closed system has tended to underestimate the importance of the birth heritage and as a result has often been lackadasical in collecting information about these vital roots. Because of the commitment to secrecy, the information that the system does manage to collect is censored and is, therefore, distorted. Since it is important in the confidential system that the two families be kept away from each other, there is no opportunity for face-to-face communication. This is a very serious liability since some of the most vital information in adoption is intangible and depends on personal contact for transmission. Given the closed system's typical assumption that birthparents and adoptive parents are natural adversaries, it is rare for data to be updated. In consummating adoptions through the closed system, then, participants typically wind up with information which is incomplete, altered, indirect, and difficult to update.

3. The third major shortcoming of the closed approach is its insistence on retaining total control of the process. This is a peculiar piece of social work since the profession almost always prefers to empower clients to take responsibility for their own lives. How odd that in this life-transforming event the major participants have so little voice! No matter how capable the participants may be, the confidential system requires that they set aside their competence and turn all the decision-making over to the agency. Such dependence ultimately invites resentment over the loss of control.

Advantages of the open system

Those attending the seminars are told that the open system addresses this power imbalance by requiring the participants to take on active and interactive roles. Recognizing that birthparents and adoptive parents are interdependent, the agency relinquishes a portion of its control to both sets of parents, thereby making it necessary for them to work together if they are to have a successful experience.

If birthparents and adoptive parents are to work together, they need to trust one another. A very crucial moment in the educational process occurs when prospective adoptive parents meet birthparents who have released children in the past. This meeting is an indispensable aid in assisting adoptive parents to overcome their fear of birthparents. They discover quite simply that birthparents are average, likeable people and they conclude that respect and support are more sensible responses than fear.

The adoptive family has a crucial opportunity to assert itself as it designs the initial portfolio of information which is used to describe them to birthparents. The sort of impression each family creates is in their own hands. It is up to them to determine which of their qualities they wish to feature. Their second major area of input is in determining how much openness they wish to offer birthparents. Although they assume a largely passive role as they wait to be chosen, they resume an active role once they are selected. In their meetings with birthparents, they will negotiate with the birthparents to design the final adoption plan. If for some reason they are uncomfortable with the birthparents or the proposed plan, the adoptive parents are free to withdraw from the arrangement. While these various decisions often take them into unfamiliar waters, most adoptive parents relish this degree of participation.

Unique appeal of the open system

Having evaluated the confidential system, the educational process shifts to its second major consideration, the unique appeal of the open system. Three major attractions for adoptive parents are highlighted: the delight of being chosen, the opportunity to experience a time of expectancy, and an enhanced sense that the child is truly theirs to parent.

1. For many years adoptive parents have told their children that they chose them from a number of possible children. This story, which pleased many adoptees during their formative years, ultimately proves unsatisfying since it is not founded in truth. Now, with open adoption, there is an honest "chosen" story, only this time it is the adoptive parents who are chosen. There is no form of flattery that can quite match being chosen in such a dramatic fashion, and adoptive parents are profoundly touched by this indication of approval and trust.

2. Since much of the adoption planning is done in the later stages of pregnancy, the chances are strong that the adoptive parents will have a chance to sample the assorted delicious anxieties associated with being expectant. Many adoptive parents, sad that their infertility denies them the chance to savor a pregnancy and birth experience, are ecstatic to be invited by birthparents to enter their journey toward delivery and share in the miraculous events surrounding birth. They enjoy making last minute preparations and laying in the necessary supplies. Many parents capitalize on the forewarning and enjoy a last night out on the town. This invitation to enter the pregnancy is a remarkable gift in its own right.

3. It is extremely important for adoptive parents to develop a sense that they are fully entitled to parent the child placed in their care. In the confidential system this can sometimes be difficult to establish since the child seems to materialize almost out of thin air. What makes it right and proper for them to take responsibility for this young stranger's life? Does the endurance required to rise to the top of a long waiting list qualify a couple to assume the awesome role of parent for a particular child? Parents who adopt through the open system have less struggle with this. By virtue of being chosen, they know that they have been invited into the child's life for good reason. Those who are able to be involved in the labor and delivery experience feel an even greater emotional connection with the baby. Although they did not physically give birth, they did participate meaningfully in the event and intensely felt the emotions of the experience.

In the open system, birthparents often invite the adoptive parents to join in the process of supplying the baby a name. This opportunity enables the new parents to enter the child's life in a meaningful and enduring manner. As they care for the baby when it is discharged from the hospital, their attachment to it intensifies and they feel that they have always been its parents. There is nothing in all the world which adds more to the adoptive parent's sense of entitlement than hearing the birthparent say, "Here, take the baby. He is yours to love. Rest assured I will never interfere." When adoptive parents know for a fact that they have the birthparent's blessing, they can relax and enjoy their parental mandate; there is no need for fear.

The risks involved

The opportunity to remedy adoption's past problems and enjoy the unique advantages of openness are available to those persons who are able to take risks. The third major component to the educational process centers on the identification of these risks and rationale for accepting them. Like the confidential system which preceded it, open adoption is far from perfect and has its share of hazards. Prospective adoptive parents need to realize that they are totally vulnerable during the two to four weeks following birth and prior to the birthparent's appearance in court for the termination of parental rights. Their fate rests with the birthparents who are, of course, completely free to change their plans. The agency instructs birthparents to completely factor the adoptive parents out of their final decision. Adoptive parents endorse the agency's posture on this, for they realize the decision must be freely reached if the openness is to work comfortably. There is little doubt that birthparents do in fact feel this freedom to alter their course, for this happens nearly twenty percent of the time—to the profound disappointment of very sincere and loving prospective parents. No one is immune from such a possibility; it can happen to anyone.

When a prospective adoptive family extends its love to a birthfamily which ultimately experiences a change of mind, the sense of loss is enormous and they must find a means to cope. Each family does this in its own way. It is not unusual for the couple to find their best support coming from their educational group, since these new friends understand the risks better than most. While there is no way around the pain, there is some comfort in recalling the reason such significant risk was taken; namely, to provide a more optimal bonding experience for the baby and to minimize unnecessary disruptions in these tender lives.

Open adoption is not an invitation to reckless living. It is important for prospective parents to be honest with themselves as they evaluate their tolerance for risk. There is no way to completely avoid risk in life, so the question each prospective parent must answer is not *whether* to risk, but rather how *much* to risk. It is a premise of open adoption that each family should decide for themselves how much risk to take rather than have the professionals decide for them. Each family must judiciously weigh the possibilities and reach their own conclusions.

There is much more involved in the educational experience, but perhaps this brief statement gives the reader some flavor of the preparations involved. Historically, many adoptive parents have viewed agency requirements as "hoops to jump through." The response to the CFCS educational program stands in stark contrast. The usual response of our adoptive parents is highly positive. Clearly, they enjoy the opportunity to reflect, learn, and grow.

Michigan adoption laws

If the reader is to fully understand the stories shared in this book, it may be helpful to briefly consider the legal requirements in Michigan which must be met for an adoption to occur. Michigan is a very unusual state because it requires that all adoptions between nonrelated persons be routed through licensed child-placing agencies. This is done to make sure that children are only placed in homes which have been evaluated and prepared for the experience of adoption. The agency approach to adoption also minimizes the financial factor so that wealthy adoptive families have no unfair advantage over those prospects with more modest means.

It is necessary in Michigan for the birthparents to appear in court to release parental rights. The court accepts the release only after it is satisfied that the birthparents make the decision on a fully informed and voluntary basis. There is no statutory timetable for this event, however. Community, Family and Children Services usually plans this hearing from two to four weeks after the child's birth. We want to give the birthmother a chance to recover from the rigors of childbirth and give both birthparents an opportunity to fully contemplate the implications of their decision, while putting some reasonable limitations on the period during which the prospective adoptive parents are at risk. During this time the baby usually resides with the chosen family as a foster child. This is a time of true emotional jeopardy for prospective adoptive families.

Following the release hearing and termination of parental rights, there is a 21-day appeal period during which the birthparents are guaranteed a hearing in an appeals court if they feel that they have been treated unfairly. The foster care arrangement remains in effect during the appeal period and is a much more relaxed time, since these appeals are very rare. When the appeal period elapses, the adoptive family is free to file their petition to adopt the child. Once the court accepts their petition, their status shifts from foster parents to adoptive parents.

During the next year the agency is required to look in on the family at least four times to assist with any adjustments they may need to make. Once the supervisory year is past, the adoption is finalized and a new birth certificate is issued. It is interesting to note that many adoptive parents are offended by the dishonesty of this new certificate which seems to rob their child of his or her biological heritage. Regardless, the remarkable process of adopting is finished. At last, the adoption is complete.

RECOMMENDED READING

Arms, Suzanne. *To Love and Let Go,* Knopf - New York - 1983

Burgess, Linda Cannon. *The Art of Adoption,* W.W. Norton - New York - 1981

Campbell, Lee H. *Understanding The Birthparent,* Concerned United Birthparents - Milford MA - 1978

Dusky, Lorraine. *Birthmark,* Evans & Company - New York - 1979

Kirk, H. David. *Shared Fate; A Theory of Adoption and Mental Health,* The Free Press - New York - 1969

Kirk, H. David. *Adoptive Kinship,* Butterworth & Company - Toronto - 1981

Krementz, Jill. *How It Feels To Be Adopted,* Knopf - New York - 1982

Lindsay, Jeanne Warren. *Open Adoption; A Caring Option,* Morning Glory Press - Buena Park CA - 1987

Lifton, Betty Jean. *Lost and Found,* Harper & Row - New York - 1988

Melina, Lois Ruskai. *Raising Adopted Children,* Harper & Row - New York - 1986

Musser, Sandra Kay. *I Would Have Searched Forever,* Haven Books - Plainfield NJ - 1979

Powledge, Fred. *The New Adoption Maze,* Mosby - St. Louis MO - 1985

Rillera, Mary Jo and Sharon Kaplan. *Cooperative Adoption,* Triadoption Publications - Westminster CA - 1984

Silber, Kathleen and Phylis Speedlin. *Dear Birthmother,* Corona Publishing Company - San Antonio TX - 1983

Sorosky, Arthur D., Annette Baran and Reuben Pannor. *The Adoption Triangle,* Doubleday Anchor Books - Garden City NY - 1979

THE ASSOCIATION
FOR OPENNESS IN ADOPTION

Many of the authors of this book are founders of an organization whose charter is to further the standards and practices of open adoption. Originally called the Michigan Association For Openness In Adoption, the organization now has a growing base of state and local chapters. The main objectives include:

1) Promoting broader public and institutional understanding and acceptance of open adoption;
2) Developing, upholding, and promoting the highest ethical standards for practices in open adoption, pregnancy counseling, and other related services;
3) Promoting research and dialogue on the impact of openness on adoption triad members and their families;
4) Serving as advocates for individuals seeking alternatives in adoption;
5) Developing and advocating approaches which can extend the benefits of openness to participants in traditional adoptions;
6) Encouraging the development of post-adoption services which focus on the life-long impact of adoption on all of the participants;
7) Supporting the efforts of individuals and organizations that work toward making adoption records accessible to all of the participants.

The Association is a sustaining co-sponsor of the National Conferences On Open Adoption—a series of international symposiums on the practice and ethics of open adoption. Many of the proceedings from past conferences are available on audio and video tape from the Association office.

The Association is a non-profit organization staffed and funded by volunteers. Inquires about membership, conferences, educational materials, speaker's bureau, donations, or other information should be directed to:

AWF Inquiry Office
The Association For
Openness In Adoption
P.O. Box 5117
Traverse City, MI 49684